WRESTLING
WITH SUCCESS

DEVELOPING A
CHAMPIONSHIP
MENTALITY

NIKITA
KOLOFF
JEFFREY
GITOMER

WILEY

JOHN WILEY & SONS, INC.

Published by John Wiley & Sons, Inc., Hoboken, New Jersey.
Published simultaneously in Canada.

Various photographs courtesy of Nikita Koloff.

For general information on our other products and services, please contact our Customer Care Department within the United States at (800) 762-2974, outside the United States at (317) 572-3993 or fax (317) 572-4002.

Wiley also publishes its books in a variety of electronic formats. Some content that appears in print may not be available in electronic books. For more information about Wiley products, visit our web site at www.Wiley.com.

Library of Congress Cataloging-in-Publication Data:

Koloff, Nikita, 1959-
  Wrestling with success : developing a championship mentality / Nikita Koloff, Jeffrey Gitomer.
    p. cm.
  ISBN 0-471-48732-5 (cloth)
  1. Success in business. 2. Success. 3. Koloff, Nikita, 1959- 4. Wrestling--Psychological aspects. I. Gitomer, Jeffrey H. II. Title.
  HF5386.K765 2004
  650.1--dc22

                                                                    2004003672

Printed in the United States of America
10 9 8 7 6 5 4 3 2 1

The secret of success is:

There's no secret of success.

This book is
dedicated to
those who
wrestle with life
and don't
quite know
how to
pin it down.

TABLE OF CONTENTS

FOREWORD
I NEVER PINNED HIM!

by

Ted DiBiase, The Million Dollar Man

When I think of Nikita Koloff my mind immediately diverts into two separate paths. My one thought is like that of many other people who are familiar with the sport of wrestling, I am sure. That is the picture of the "Russian Nightmare" standing in mid-ring with his hand raised after vanquishing another opponent amidst the awestruck legions of fans. The other is that of my long-time and most valued friend, with whom I have traveled countless miles since we have both left the battles of the ring.

The world of professional wrestling is full of unusual and colorful characters. As the "Million Dollar Man," I've pretty much met them all. I learned through my many years in the wrestling business that a real man is not measured by his physical stature or by the championship belt around his waist but by his integrity and the willingness to keep his word, no matter the cost. Nikita Koloff is such a man.

It is ironic, considering the decades we've spent traveling the world facing countless adversaries night after night, that Nikita and my paths never crossed in the ring. I do recall meeting him briefly in Atlanta when I was working for World Championship Wrestling and he was visiting Animal, of the Road Warriors, who was a friend of his. It was nothing more than a brief handshake and a few words, if that. His visage did not denote the havoc-wreaking machine from the Soviet Union, but one of a young athlete like so many others I had met, complete with the blow-dried, feathered hair of the disco era.

A few years later, I kept hearing of this giant Russian carving a large path throughout the Mid-Atlantic territory. At 6 feet 2 inches tall and 285 pounds, Nikita cast a menacing figure. Later I learned that this man that seemed invincible in the ring and that couldn't speak any English was the same kid with the perfect hair I had met a few years earlier. Only Nikita could have pulled that off.

You may be wondering what all this has to do with developing a championship mentality and succeeding no matter what the obstacles, but if you take a closer look at what it takes to succeed, you will see a strong correlation. What Nikita did in the ring is the same thing that he, I, and others have put to work in successful ventures outside of the ring.

It doesn't matter what you are striving for in life. Whether it be in athletics, education, family, or business the same tenets apply and the path to success is always the same. It starts with the ability to set goals and to say "here is where I want to go and I am willing to make whatever sacrifice necessary to achieve it." Next, it takes the courage to make a commitment to those ends, and finally, the will to follow through until you succeed.

I believe that you cannot truly experience the joy of success until you have felt the pain of failure. There is no shame in failure, but there is in refusing to try. In fact, most of the successful people I know have had many failures along the way, but they were willing to take risks. Nikita knows this well, so listen closely.

Nikita explains in this book that success comes by doing little things and in that you will find success in the larger things you wish to achieve. It may not be easy, but more games are won by racking up base hits than by hitting grand slams.

After I graduated from West Texas State University, I entered professional wrestling, not at the top but as a preliminary wrestler. My job was to lose. And lose I did, every night to everyone I faced. I knew my time would come, so I not only had to be patient but I had to be ready when it came. We would wrestle in Shreveport, Louisiana on Tuesday night and the top stars would stay over to do interviews for their upcoming matches on television the next day. Then we would have to drive as many as 300 miles afterward to the next match. I would also stay, not to do interviews (after all, who would want to listen to a guy who gets beaten every night?), but to listen to those who were interviewed and to take notes.

I was a long way from the main event, but I knew that when I finally made it I would have the skills I would need to be successful. Yes, it was a sacrifice to drive all afternoon to the next town. Many times I barely made it before the opening bell, but it was more than worth it. There is always a price to be paid, and as Nikita spells out in the ensuing pages, if you are willing to pay it you will find many successes in your future.

This is not just another book on business and success philosophy, but a practical guide written by a man who accomplished tremendous goals by overcoming nearly every obstacle imaginable. Pay close attention and don't be afraid to put these ideas into practice for yourself. You will be most glad that you did.

TO BUY -- OR NOT TO BUY!
TO READ -- OR NOT TO READ!
TO WRESTLE -- OR NOT TO WRESTLE!
Why is this book for you? -- or not for you.

Everybody thinks professional wrestling is fixed -- and everybody is wrong. Including you!

The outcomes are predetermined. Just because I knew how the match would end, didn't mean I didn't have to get ready to win.

The secret to your success is predetermining **your** outcomes.

You are looking for the secret to success -- and I found it -- and I'm going to share it. All you have to do is read until you find the AHA! for yourself.

Success is about many things and comes in many forms.
Success is about failure.
Success is about getting ready.
Success is about predetermined outcomes.

I have been a champion athlete.
I have been a champion in professional wrestling.
And I have been a champion at professional business.
All those championships have everything in common.

You don't have to be a professional wrestler to be a success, but you do have to wrestle: with yourself, with your self-discipline, with your desires, with your passion, with your attitude, with your belief, and with your spirituality.

IS THIS A BOOK ABOUT PROFESSIONAL WRESTLING?

It's way better than that. Sure, there's a bunch of interesting stories about the real and surreal world of professional wrestling. But more important, it takes those stories and examples and shows you what you can learn from wrestling and convert it to your own success.

Not many people get to be a professional wrestler. In fact, not many people even watch professional wrestling (anymore). But you all know what professional wrestling is: soap opera for men.

Here's what you don't know about professional wrestling:

Professional wrestling is **preparation**.
Professional wrestling is **acting**.
Professional wrestling is **athleticism**.
Professional wrestling is **coordination**.
Professional wrestling is **training**.
Professional wrestling is **timing**.
Professional wrestling is **concentration**.
Professional wrestling is **selling**.
Professional wrestling is **"getting over."**

Professional wrestling is an example of what it will take for anyone (you included) to become a success. And in this book you will begin to understand how to convert those lessons to your success and your life.

This is a championship match. Your mind vs. the world. You are the challenger and the challenged. And here's the cool part -- at the end of this book, you win!

I Hate You!

"I booed the bad guy; I cheered the good guy. I was a fan. A real fan."

-- *Jeffrey Gitomer*

All meetings are by some degree of chance or serendipity. Some would say by design.

Eight years ago I was attending the annual Chamber of Commerce business expo to see my friend Harvey Mackay deliver the keynote address.

Gitomer

A friend of mine came running over to me and said, "Aren't you a wrestling fan?" "Of course," I replied, "isn't everyone?" My friend kind of frowned but added, "You know that big Russian wrestler Nikita Koloff? He's right around the corner at one of the booths!"

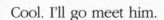

Koloff

Cool. I'll go meet him.

"Hi, my name is Jeffrey Gitomer. I'm the guy that writes the column every week in the *Charlotte Business Journal*," I said with hand extended.

"I read your column all the time. I'm a big fan. My name is Nikita Koloff," he said with hand extended.

"I've hated your guts for ten years," I said, hoping he wouldn't slug me.

"I guess it worked," he said with a smile.

We talked for about thirty minutes, twenty-nine of which fulfilled my wrestling fantasies. I asked him everything about everyone, and he knew all the answers. Plus he was a nice guy. I mean a real nice guy. We agreed to meet later.

And we've been meeting for the past eight years.

What I've learned from Nikita is that his experiences led him to his success. And while he may not have had a game plan along the way, his preparation, his self-discipline, and his ability to think quickly on his feet enabled him to capture opportunities as they arose.

"Gonna write a book?" I asked him one day a few years ago. "Someday," he replied.

"That's what everyone says who never writes a book," I snapped. "There are huge parallels between preparation in sports and preparation in business. Both require hard work and dedication. Both lead to success, or better said, create winners. Wanna write a book together?"

"That would be great," he said. "No," I said. "That would be work."

And it has been a labor of love and inspiration. And so will it be for you.

TWO AUTHORS. ONE GOAL.

Nikita Koloff will share his story and his success principles throughout the course of this book. He is the actual writer of his own material. Most athletes who write a book have a ghost writer who writes everything. This book is different. You actually get to read the thoughts of the author.

Jeffrey Gitomer will share his insights and his success principles. He is a world-class writer, a world-class thinker, and THE world-class salesman.

Wherever there's a doubt as to who wrote what, we will try to identify Koloff and Gitomer with their names.

But to you the reader, it's not as important who wrote it as how that information applies to you and how you can use it for your own success.

WHAT YOU WILL FIND AS YOU READ THIS BOOK

This book is divided into six parts. Each of them contains specific information that will lead you from one to the other. You can't start at the end. You have to read this book page by page. Same way with success. Step by step.

This book is full of cool stuff.

> There is the Nikita Koloff story of wrestling.
>
> There is the Nikita Koloff story of business.
>
> There is the Nikita Koloff story of success.
>
> There is the Nikita Koloff story of life.
>
> There are insights and wisdom that will help turn these stories into your realities.

Pin down success. At the end of each chapter you'll find a 1-2-3 count. These are not just summaries; they are insights and challenges so you can come to an understanding of how to convert what has been said to your victory.

There are quotes from people who wrestled and quotes from wimps (people who didn't wrestle). The quotes are there to provide an additional thought process. If you decide to put one on your computer or send one to someone else, please be sure to acknowledge the author as we did.

There is a story line that is threaded throughout the book. As you read it, you'll begin to catch the addiction of professional wrestling as it was in the mid-1980s, what we would refer to as the "heyday" of wrestling.

Nikita as the U.S. heavyweight champion in 1985.

And you will find a cornucopia of ideas, strategies, and gems that you can take to the bank. Your bank.

And of course, at the end of the success championship battle, you win the fight and get the belt.

"… and in this corner, from parts unknown …"

FROM FEAR TO NO FEAR

"I can be more than I am now."

-- *Nikita Koloff*

My 11-year-old daughter asked me if I had ever been afraid. She told me she never felt afraid or threatened in school and asked me if I had ever experienced that. I told her there was one time in elementary school, the last year before I moved out of the projects. I would never forget it. During a bathroom break, I was left in the bathroom with the two school bullies.

I was never an aggressive person. I was always very shy and very quiet to the point where most people thought I was stuck up. I really just wasn't much of a conversationalist. But in the bathroom, I guess it was my turn for the bullies to pick on me. They said, "After school, someone will meet you outside to beat you up." I remember thinking for the rest of the day about my escape route home from school. In those days we walked home, no buses. First I had to figure out how to avoid this after school today, but how would I avoid it tomorrow, and the next day, and the next day?

I slipped out of school and sprinted six blocks back to my house. My friend Edwin was known as the tough guy in school, and fortunately for me, he was my best friend. I told him what had happened, and he said, "Don't worry, I'll take care of it." I knew if Edwin said it, it would be done. So the next school day, he went and set the record straight with the two bullies. After that, I never had any fears for the rest of the school year.

This event triggered my first thoughts of "When am I going to get out of here? How are we going to get out of here?" After the fourth grade, my mother was able to move us out of the ghetto and into the suburbs a week before the new school year started. Even though we had moved out of the ghetto, we didn't move out of the welfare bracket. I was still fatherless, the youngest of four, and still on welfare.

As a kid in a new neighborhood, I didn't know anyone yet, and I had to ride the school bus for the first time. The walk down the street to get to the bus was only a block, but it seemed like a hundred miles. I was afraid, but I overcame that fear, made friends, and soon became popular among the neighborhood kids.

Nikita at Moorhead State University, 1981.

When I was 12, I picked up a muscle magazine called *Ironman* with a lot of bodybuilders in it. I'm not sure why I picked it up, but I did. I began to read and look at the pictures and articles. Not long after that, not more than hours or days, I had a vision that I could look like those guys in the magazine. So I got a paper route to earn my own income so I could buy some weights.

From the money I earned from my paper route, I bought a 110-pound weight set and kept it in my garage. Around this time, I began to develop an attitude that "I can be more than I am now." For whatever reason, I was identifying with the guys in the magazines. I began to envision the body, the muscles, and I knew that one day I could and would look like those guys.

I had always liked football and started to watch the NFL on television more and more. I tossed the football around a lot with the neighborhood kids. We would play street football in the rain, shine, or frozen snow-packed asphalt of the streets. In Minnesota, even in

Robbinsdale High School, Robbinsdale, MN, 1977. Perseverance and hard work begin sculpting a championship form.

below-zero weather, we were out there playing. Our mentality was, "If the Minnesota Vikings could do it, so could we."

Not long after watching football on television, I began to envision myself playing in the NFL. I figured out that if I wanted to play in the NFL, I couldn't just watch it on television and wait for the Vikings to call. I had to take action. I had to join a team, study the play book, and learn the game.

I always had the vision before I had the achievement.

THE "I'M GONNA" FACTOR

I'm gonna write a book.
I'm gonna read that book.
I'm gonna lose some weight.
I'm gonna quit smoking.
I'm gonna take that course.
I'm gonna start that tomorrow.
I'm gonna, I'm gonna, I'm gonna ...

"What's the hardest part about writing a book?" This question was asked of my co-author, the Great Nikita Koloff. "Getting started," Nikita shared with someone at a luncheon before he headed off to Charlotte, North Carolina, to complete this book project. The person replied, "Oh, the first chapter?" And Nikita said, "No, the first sentence."

Koloff: How many things have you wanted to do but never did? It's my hope this book will help you overcome the "roll over" factor, and the "I'm gonna" factor which will then lead you to say, "I accomplished the 'I did it' factor."

Gitomer: How many things have you ever wanted to do in your life that you thought were great ideas, but you never started? That's a tough question. But let me ask you a tougher one. What would it take for you to get started? That is the $64,000 question (for those of you old enough to remember).

I rarely quote other people but this one deserves it, "A journey of 1,000 miles begins with a single step." Lao-tzu. Millions of people have millions of intentions and millions of ideas and millions of brainstorms and millions of goals and millions of sales calls and millions of follow-ups where the first step is never taken.

How many of them have you had? Answer: too many.

There are 2.5 factors that play a primary role in taking the first step. One is the *roll over factor*. Two is the *I'm gonna factor*. And 2.5 is the *I did it factor*.

1. The roll over factor deals with your personal self-discipline and your personal dedication and lies somewhere between just getting things done and personal excellence. Your alarm clock goes off. You hit the *snooze* button and you roll over. And the alarm goes off again. And you hit the *snooze* button again and roll over. And the alarm goes off again. Only this time you hit the *off* button and roll over. You're thinking to yourself each time, "I really ought to get up, but I just don't feel like it."

> ## "Oh, sluggard, how long will you sleep?"
>
> *-- The Book of Proverbs*

The roll over factor is the easiest one to explain because each of you has done it no less than a hundred times (in the last year). You know you gotta do it. You know you should do something. You've been thinking about doing it. You made a goal to do it. And it ain't getting done, baby. Many of you have gotten out of bed and still didn't do it.

Gitomer: At one point in my life I considered myself a runner. I would wake up in the morning, most of the time before the sun came up, put on my running clothes according to the weather, and go out for a jog. Two miles, three miles, four miles, sometimes more. I never came back from a run where I didn't feel great (by the way, running doesn't help you live longer, it just seems longer). But every run started with my self-discipline and my desire for personal excellence to **take the first step.**

And then I quit. Hey, I had a good excuse (just like you do). I'm busy, I gotta speak, I gotta write, I gotta make a sale, I got appointments, I gotta catch a plane. Whatever the excuse is, they all have the same definition: **LAME.** And now it's up to me to return to those thrilling days of yesteryear when the Lone Ranger rides (er, runs) again. Hi ho, fat boy. I gotta shed twenty pounds of unwanted fat.

The only way that it will get done is if I decide to do something about it and then take the first step. Just like you.

2. The I'm gonna factor. The step-child of "roll over" is "I'm gonna." I'm gonna lose some weight. I'm gonna quit smoking. I'm gonna read that book. I'm gonna take that course. I'm gonna write that book. I'm gonna start that business. I'm gonna achieve that goal. And then you never take the first step.

One of the main reasons that people don't take the first step is that they have no plan and no vision of the outcome. And they haven't figured out what benefits they would enjoy as a result of achieving the success. For reasons too many to list, the best thing to do is: **list your own reasons.** Take a moment and make yourself more determined (maybe even angry) by listing the reasons (excuses) that you have failed to take the first step.

Pretty pathetic, huh? Any real good ones? I can tell you for a fact that mine stink. I have no good reasons for not exercising. I have no good reasons for not eating better. I have no good reasons for not staying healthier. Oh, I have a hundred excuses. But not one good reason. Neither do you.

The good news is every human being suffers from the *I'm gonna factor*. The better news is, if you want to differentiate yourself from the sluggard, all you have to do is develop a deeper self-discipline, a deeper desire, a deeper determination, and a game plan to begin combined with a celebration of victory at the end. The best news is that if you do take the first step, you'll be in the minority. At the top.

Which leads me to **2.5,** the **I did it! factor.** For years I have preached in sales that the easiest time to make a sale is right after you just made one because you are on a roll. You're in that euphoric state of achievement. You did it!

The secret to taking the first step is to visualize previous first steps combined with the feeling you got when you were victorious. That's the beginning of your self-confidence, your self-determination, and your desire to take the first step. You can do it.

Gonna read this book?
Take the first step …
turn the page!

Let's get ready to ruuuummmble!

"Everyone wants to be a champion
-- do you have what it takes?"

Part

1

Getting Ready

The Boy Scout motto,
"Be Prepared,"
is something that
each of you knows,
but very few of you
comply with.

That's the challenge.
And that's the
opportunity
for success.

Get ready!

Chapter  1

THE GHETTO --
A VERY BRIEF HISTORY

"There are two ways of meeting
difficulties; you may alter the difficulty
or you may alter yourself meeting it."

-- *Phyllis Bottome*

It was called low-income housing by the politically correct. We, the
inhabitants, called it the ghetto, or the projects.

I found myself living in this setting because my mother was left to
raise four children on her own, of which I was the youngest. It
was the 1960s and we had a balanced mixture of white and black
families in my neighborhood. As time progressed, more and more
of the white families moved to the suburbs.

I grew up in an era when prejudice was very prevalent in America,
but not with me. Motown music became my favorite to listen to and
Muhammad Ali was my favorite athlete. Some of my best friends
were black, one of whom was Edwin, although I called him Etwin
because I couldn't pronounce his name correctly. (It wasn't due to a
speech impediment -- I just had trouble pronouncing it!) He was my
best friend. Although I have limited memories of those early years,
they are fond memories.

Though tough to describe the buildings themselves, I wouldn't
exactly call them row houses like in Philadelphia, and they certainly
weren't town houses as you know them today. They were more like
apartment units, six of them attached together, brick-built, two-story.

We lived in one of the middle units. The youngest of four, I shared a bedroom with my oldest brother, eleven years older, my sister shared a bedroom with my mom, and my other brother got the last bedroom.

My oldest brother was an athlete and definitely had an influence on me. He would always tell me, "If you're gonna be an athlete, you can't smoke or drink alcohol." I took those words to heart.

Minneapolis was a very clean city and still is to this day. There wasn't much crime in the projects that I was aware of at this stage in life. We were very close to downtown Minneapolis. In fact, I could see the skyline from the front door of my house (as I called it).

One of my not-so-fond memories of childhood happened one hot summer day as the older kids were having a waterhose fight in the common area. We younger kids would run through the water to cool off. I thought it was my turn to run through the water, and another young guy thought the same thing. He came from the opposite direction, and we collided heads with one another. Nothing happened to him other than getting knocked down, but unfortunately for me, I had split my skull wide open.

I was rushed to the hospital and received more stitches than I care to remember. The doctor shaved a big patch of hair off the top of my head and fastened a large, white bandage to it. It was the most embarrassing moment of my life up to that time. I didn't even want to leave my house, and when I had to, I wore a cap on my head.

I am very grateful and thankful for my humble beginnings. I learned very early in life the value of a dollar and how to spend money wisely.

In the summer of 1969 I was ten, and we made "the big move" to the suburbs. We were the second-to-last white family to leave the ghetto. Apprehensive about my new surroundings, I learned to adapt. In fact, within a year, I would begin my career as an entrepreneur, securing a position as a delivery boy for the *Minneapolis Star and Tribune* newspaper.

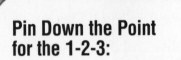

Pin Down the Point
for the 1-2-3:

1. You start where your parents put you.

2. You are a product of your environment and your associations until you get a clue.

3. Start working (hard) as soon as you can.

My intensity convinced them to believe.

Chapter  2

SOMEONE SAID, "BREAK A LEG" -- SO I DID. (VISION SHATTERED.)

INJURY BREEDS DETERMINATION -- A STORY OF OPPORTUNITY, NOT TRAGEDY.

> "The best thing about the future is that it comes only one day at a time."
> *-- Abraham Lincoln, former wrestler*

As an eighteen-year-old punk kid, I found myself lying on the football field in Thief River Falls, Minnesota, with a shattered leg. During a football game my freshman year of college, a pass play was intended to come to me. The whistle was blown, I turned around to see why, and a player on my team was shoved into me.

He hit me below the knee, and it sounded like a dry twig snapping in half. I heard it plain as day but didn't know what it was until I actually looked down and saw what had happened. The bones in my leg between my knee and ankle formed the shape of the letter Z. I later found out that I broke my tibia and fibula bones completely in half.

As an eighteen-year-old lying on the field, all I could think of was, "Why me?" I remember thinking that my career was shattered because my bones were shattered. My dream as a youngster to play in the NFL was shattered, literally and figuratively.

I spent the next seventeen days flat on my back in a hospital bed, trying to contemplate the future.

Friends can play an integral role in your success or failure. They can either say things to encourage you or discourage you. Just read the story of Job (in the Old Testament). I was fortunate enough to have a friend who supported me. He visited me every day, sometimes twice a day, during the seventeen days I was in the hospital, and he continued to visit me after I got out. His name was Tim Peltier. As much encouragement and support as he gave me, it took a former high school coach's comment to become the driving force and motivation to make me decide to return to the football field. He said to me, "I heard about your injury. That's too bad. Nobody has ever come back from an injury like that."

I thought to myself, "Is that right, pal? I'll show you. Not only will I come back, I will be a starter again." And I did.

I rehabilitated the leg with that comment in my mind the entire time. It gave me the determination to get back out there. Never let somebody else's opinion of you become your reality. You hear them every day from parents, siblings, friends, teachers, coaches, and co-workers. They mold you and shape you into who you are. But you don't have to believe it.

It's been said a fool has no delight in understanding, but in expressing his own opinion. It's all in how you receive it. In my mind, I used my coach's opinion as motivation and determination to come back.

I went through rehabilitation, recovered, came back, earned a starting position, and continued with my college career. I was having an extremely successful senior season when my dream was interrupted for the second time. But this time it was to the other leg. An identical fracture, four years later, to the opposite leg. Same scenario.

It was a beautiful, sunny afternoon, my pass play was called, I caught the ball, and there was nothing between me and the end zone but green grass. And then I saw it. The shadow of my opponent who was behind me chasing me down. As I turned upfield, he was just able to grab my jersey and pull me back. And once again, I heard the sound of a dry twig snapping. Only this time I knew what had happened. The kicker is, I was being scouted by the NFL. They were there in the stands, watching the whole thing happen.

When I first found out that the scouts were coming, I was literally seeing my dreams fulfilled. To a youngster dreaming of playing in the NFL, it is still not a reality until you get a call, or they knock on your door, or the coach calls you to tell you the scouts are here to watch you. That's when the dream becomes a reality. And I had had this happen to me. My coach called me and said, "Come down to the field house, I have some guys here that want to meet you." Looking back, even at that point, even if I had never made the NFL, the fact that they had the interest and took the time and expense to come out and scout me, to me, was a victory in itself.

I went from being an eighteen-year-old punk kid lying on the field wondering why me, my life shattered, to being encouraged and motivated by friends and coaches, to the reality of rehabilitating and starting again, and developing the attitude and mentality that I am back on track, I can make it to the NFL.

So, dream shattered, round two. However, that was the opportunity. At eighteen, my mentality was life was over, now what? As a college senior, I told myself, "This is okay, I have been here before, I have come back from this before, and I will come back and play in the NFL." Just knowing they had come to scout me, I knew I had what it took to overcome it and be a success. I had proven myself already; I knew I could do it again.

And so began the process of a year and a half of rehabilitation. Eight hours a day in the gym to prepare myself for an NFL tryout. I was developing my championship mentality.

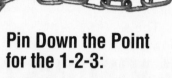

Pin Down the Point
for the 1-2-3:

1. Someone else's opinion does not have to become your reality. When something breaks your dreams, the sooner you realize it's not the end of the world, the better chance you have of turning the obstacle into an opportunity.

2. The more you mope, the less you see what life has in store for you. Moping blocks vision.

3. Friends cannot do it for you, but they sure can reassure you that you can.

Chapter  3

CREATING VISIONS AND BEING WILLING TO WIN

"People who try to do something and fail
are infinitely better than those who try to
do nothing and succeed."

-- Anonymous

"A vision without a task is a dream, a
task without a vision is drudgery; the two
combined make for success."

-- Nikita Koloff

I picked up an *Ironman* magazine, flipped through page after page
of muscle-bound men, and envisioned myself looking like one of
those guys. But I realized I couldn't just look at the magazine and
become like that. I had to take action. I had to get in the gym. I had
to lift the weights. I had to dedicate myself. And because I did, I
was able to build myself into a 285-pound behemoth with 8 percent
body fat and a 34-inch waist.

When I started watching the NFL, I had a vision that one day I
would play in the NFL. But I realized I couldn't just watch the game
on television and wait for the Minnesota Vikings to call me up when
I was of age and tell me they were ready for me to join their team.
If I was going to play in the NFL, I had to learn the game. I had to
join a team. I had to study the playbook.

Fighting Ric Flair in 1986.

And I wasn't content just being part of the team. I didn't envision myself sitting on the bench, or standing on the sidelines cheering the other guys on. I saw myself in the starting lineup. I wanted to be catching touchdown passes. I wanted to be sacking the quarterback. I wanted to be the best. Because of hard work and determination, this vision became more of a reality when the NFL scouts showed up on my college campus and put me through a battery of NFL tests.

When I broke into professional wrestling, I wasn't content just being another wrestler. I wasn't satisfied calling my family and friends saying, "Hey, watch me on Saturday night on TBS because I'm going to be wrestling." I wanted to be, and I was determined to be, a world champion. I wanted to be the best. And through hard work and determination, I became a world champion many times over.

Each of these experiences taught me some valuable lessons in life. Having a vision is one thing. Being willing to win is another. But I wouldn't have accomplished either had I not taken action.

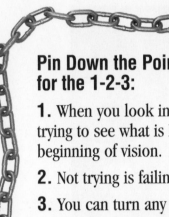

Pin Down the Point for the 1-2-3:

1. When you look in the mirror, often you're trying to see what is **NOT** there. That's the beginning of vision.

2. Not trying is failing.

3. You can turn any dream into reality by envisioning it every day and taking some small step to achieve it.

World champion. Dream achieved.

Chapter  **4**

TWO PARTS OF WORKING OUT: LIFTING AND HANGING

"Time is the one thing that can never be retrieved. Hours lost in idleness can never be brought back to be used in gainful pursuits."

-- C.R. Lawton

Not many guys can wear a girlie boa wrap and get away with it. Actually make a fashion statement with it. Actually develop a reputation from it. Actually become a success as a result of it. Actually get elected governor of Minnesota in spite of it.

Jesse Ventura – love him or hate him – predetermined his success with preparation. In addition to his physical stature and time in the gym, Jesse was blessed with an intangible ability to carry himself before an audience as well as the television camera. I believe his success in becoming governor was directly connected to his experiences in wrestling. His ability to communicate in front of the camera to his audiences for wrestling prepared him well for politics. His charisma and comfort level were well-established. His opponents didn't stand a chance as history now proves.

As a youth, I worked out in his gym. So did "Ravishing" Rick Rude, Barry Darsow (aka Krusher Krushchev), John Nord (aka The

A touch of insanity never hurts to make it in pro wrestling.

Barbarian), "Mr. Perfect" Curt Hennig, and about twenty other muscle heads.

Jesse would sit behind the front desk rocking in his chair and carrying on a conversation with us. I guess we gravitated toward him because his attitude was similar to the attitude we carried. I'll never forget how he would ask our opinions as to what he should say for his television interviews, and sometimes he would use our suggestions. That was pretty cool! Little did I know at the time that I would one day end up in the same profession as "The Body," or now better known as "The Mind."

Jesse was in the latter part of his wrestling career by the time I broke into the business. But he spent several more years in the industry as a color commentator. It was fun to get to know him in the gym, but it paled in comparison to working with him side by side in the wrestling industry. Because of our shaved heads and similar looks, people often mistake us for each other. Jesse once told me how people always ask him, "Are you Nikita Koloff?", and

Baron von Rasche teams up with the Russians in 1984. In order to succeed, you must surround yourself with successful people.

he would answer "What, do I look like, some Russian?" And to this day, people still ask me if I'm Jesse. We've continued our friendship, usually running into each other at "The Gym" in Minnesota.

As important as the lifting was, hanging with Jesse at the gym was even more important. I didn't realize it at the time, but looking back twenty years later, he definitely had an influence on my success as a wrestler. Just being around him and watching his interviews on the All-Star Wrestling program gave me insights for my own character.

In order for you to improve your chances for success, you must hang around better people. People who have more knowledge than you, more wisdom than you, are financially better off than you. Don't hang around people who say, "You have a good job. Why are you going into wrestling?" or "Why are you starting your own business? Are you crazy?" or "You're running for governor? You're kidding, right?"

So let me ask you a question, who are you working out with? Who are you hanging out with? You may have to reevaluate the people you are surrounding yourself with if you want to be more successful.

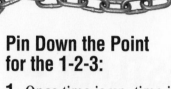

Pin Down the Point for the 1-2-3:

1. Once time is up, time is up! Your time is your most valuable asset -- you must choose how to invest it. Most people take it for granted and waste it. You can be ahead of all those people by making a time plan and valuing your time the same way you value your bank account. How are you investing your time?

2. People you surround yourself with can determine who and what you become. Who are you hanging around with?

3. You never know who is going to be governor. Build friendships and keep them. Who are your friends?

Chapter  5

WRESTLING --
A VERY BRIEF HISTORY

"In no channel has the world stood still.
Whether it be science or any other
achievement, the world moves forward.
Anything that does not improve, dies
after a time."

-- *William Muldoon, former wrestler*

HISTORY OF WRESTLING

The roots of wrestling actually go back to the 1870s post–Civil War
era. Some of the first heavyweight champions were Frank Gotch,
George Hackenschmidt, and "Strangler" Ed Lewis. Former president
Teddy Roosevelt was quoted one time as saying, "If I can't be the
president, then I'd like to be George Hackenschmidt, the world
wrestling champion."

One of the first matches was at an opera house in New York.
It began as a competition and eventually migrated to the early
carnivals. One of the highlights of the evening was the open
challenge to the audience for anyone to come into the ring and
wrestle the champion, which led to some tough matches and stiff
competition. Somewhere along that timeline, the carnival promoters
began grooming more guys to be wrestlers and putting them in
competition with each other. Eventually it evolved from the big tent
at the carnival to the armories, high school gyms, and other venues.

photo by Russell Lee

Wrestling match sponsored by the American Legion in Sikeston, Missouri, 1938.

The promoters realized that the more interesting the characters involved, the greater the interest from the fans. So they began to develop characters such as Haystacks Calhoun, Lou Thesz, Man Mountain Mike, Wild Samoans, and Handsome Harley Race. Then they added flamboyant characters like Gorgeous George, Nature Boy Buddy Rogers, Nature Boy Ric Flair, Superstar Billy Graham, American Dream Dusty Rhodes, Hulk Hogan, The Million Dollar Man Ted DiBiase, The Heartbreak Kid Shawn Michaels and The Rock. Eventually foreign characters, such as Bruno Samartino, became a huge success among the Italian-American population. Other foreign characters played off the signs of the times, such

photo by Chicago Daily News, Inc.

George Hackenschmidt poses in a 1908 photograph.

as the Russian Nightmare Nikita Koloff, the Russian Bear Ivan Koloff (the Cold War between America and the former Soviet Union), the Iron Sheik (the first Gulf War), Sergeant Slaughter and Corporal Don Kernodle, the American Heroes, and the Road Warriors, whose character development came from the movie

Mad Max. The promoters took advantage of current affairs, politics, and movies of the time and created these characters.

As wrestling continued to evolve, it went from the high school gyms and armories, to the big arenas, to the mainstream via television. It initially grew in popularity because of regional television, and then advanced to national television programming

photo by Jack Delano

Wrestlers at the Tunbridge World's Fair in Tunbridge, Vermont, 1941.

via cable, to worldwide exposure and development via the satellite, and to the explosion on pay-per-view. That was what brought it the mainstream popularity that it has today.

Because of the caliber athlete that the pro wrestler has become, along with their acting abilities, many have crossed over into other arenas such as the movie industry or television shows, (sometimes even hosting their own programs). And let's not forget the manufacturing and marketing of their likenesses by hundreds of companies worldwide, producing things like lunch boxes, video games, bedsheets, and countless other novelties. A good friend of mine, Steve Borden, better known as Sting, had three hundred to four hundred companies producing his likeness around the world.

The success of the character totally depended upon the ability of the wrestler. His abilities both in the ring and in front of the camera were critical to his rise to stardom. The key was to build the character, his recognition, his brand, and how people perceived him -- good guy or bad guy. Success would then lie in the approval or disapproval, or the cheers and boos, of the fans.

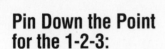

Pin Down the Point
for the 1-2-3:

1. Life is going to go by with or without you. You decide how much of a difference you want to make.

2. Almost everything on television is about other people's dramas. How is watching television helping your character?

3. Your success is all about the small building blocks that you use as your own foundation. Your success is all about your decisions as they relate to the opportunities that lie in front of you. It's not about other people. It's not about the weather. It's not about the television. It may not even be about your job. It's about your preparation, your perception, your persistence, your performance, and your passion.

Chapter  6

NIKITA KOLOFF IS BORN WITHOUT ME BEING THERE.

"To be the man, you have to beat the
man … and walk that aisle, baby."

-- *Ric Flair, Nature Boy*

Timing is everything. In 1984 the Olympics were being held in Los
Angeles, California. Most people thought that the Soviet Union
would boycott the games because the United States had boycotted
the games in Moscow in 1980. Don Kernodle and Sergeant
Slaughter were wrestling in the World Wrestling Federation (WWF)
at the time and conceived an idea to develop a Russian character,
or nephew, for the legendary "Russian Bear" Ivan Koloff.

This partner was supposed to have competed in the Olympics that
year but couldn't because of the boycott. Ivan was to bring his
"nephew" across the sea and turn him pro so he didn't have to wait
another four years for the next Olympics.

Here was the idea: First, Don would leave the WWF and head
south to the National Wrestling Alliance (NWA) and become Ivan's
tag-team partner as an American turncoat. They would become
the world tag-team champions. Ivan's "nephew" would then enter
the scene. The three of them would become the world six-man
champions as well. Eventually, Ivan and his nephew (as only
Russians could do) would turn against Don. This would switch
Don from being a "bad guy" to a "good guy."

If the plan was done right, the switch would generate huge dollars at the box office. Don presented the idea to Jim Crockett, promoter of the NWA's Mid-Atlantic wrestling organization, who loved the idea.

What Ivan and I ended up doing with Don came off as one of the best angles in the wrestling business. Here's how it worked: Don and Ivan (the champions) wrestled The Rock 'n' Roll Express (the challengers) for the world titles. Ivan and Don lost the belts, and Ivan blamed Don for the loss. As the crowd roared in excitement, I ran The Rock 'n' Roll Express out of the ring, which left Ivan, Don, and me alone in the ring.

Still reeling from getting pinned for the 1-2-3, I attacked Don. Ivan joined in, and we beat him to a bloody pulp. I got my chain and told Ivan to hoist him up on his shoulders. I climbed to the top rope and lunged off, hit Don with the Russian Sickle and the chain at the same time.

He did a 180-degree flip and crashed down on the mat. He lay motionless in the center of the ring. Other wrestlers began to enter the ring, to come to his aid and to run Ivan and me off. Don's parents were attending that night and came to the ring, as well as his brother (who wrestled as Rocky Kernodle).

Teamwork breeds success.

Unplanned, a nurse from Atlanta was in the stands and came to assist the paramedics. They put a neck brace on him, carried him out on a stretcher, and took him to the hospital in an ambulance. Don later told me how the same people who had cussed him, spat on him, and booed him were now telling him how much they loved him. He said about three hundred fans showed up at the hospital.

The doctors wanted to keep him overnight because the nurse from Atlanta told the doctors he was unconscious when she got into the ring. Cold and hungry, Don had to convince the doctors to let him go home.

The angle could not have come off any better. In viewing the video afterwards, it really looked like we killed him.

At the next match, it was time for Don to call in the cavalry. He said, "There is only one man I could get as a partner to defeat these dirty Russians and that would be Sergeant Slaughter."

Now there was the classic Cold War matchup of the Americans and the American flag vs. the Russians and the Soviet flag.

To set up this "turn," Don left the WWF, headed to the NWA, became Ivan's tag-team partner, and with him won the world tag-team titles. Needless to say, Don was tremendously hated by the fans for his alliance with the Russian Bear.

The story line couldn't have developed any better. As they were conceiving the idea, Don approached Joe Laurinaitis, better known as Road Warrior Animal of the Legion of Doom and asked, "Do you know a big guy like yourself who isn't doing anything and wouldn't mind becoming a Russian and shaving his head?"

Without hesitation Animal said, "I know just the guy. Let me make a call."

Pin Down the Point for the 1-2-3:

1. You never know how much preparation it takes until you find yourself in an opportunity and you are unprepared.

2. Success starts with an opportunity.

3. It's not who you know, it's who you know who they know.

Part

2

Being Ready

OPPORTUNITY IS A WORD THAT MOST PEOPLE DO NOT UNDERSTAND.

When it shows up,
most people are
unprepared for it.
Then they labor over
the decision,
"Should I or shouldn't I?"

The more you question
the opportunity,
the less prepared
you probably are.

In this section of the book, you will learn the importance of being ready to seize the opportunity when it occurs. You will journey with Nikita as he storms the squared circle, and you will see that his preparation was the key element for his victory.

Chapter  7

THE PHONE RANG; IT WAS THE ANIMAL.

"WHAT DO YOU THINK ABOUT WRESTLING?" THE STORY OF "HOW I GOT INTO WRESTLING."

"Things may come to those who wait.
But only the things left by those
who hustle."

-- Abraham Lincoln, former wrestler

The phone rang at my home in Robbinsdale at 9 a.m. in April 1984.
It was The Animal. The Road Warrior Animal. I recruited The Animal
for our college football team at Golden Valley Lutheran College. He
came, and we became the best of friends. Brothers. His family took
me in as their prodigal son in 1978.

That April morning, Animal said to me, "What do you think about
wrestling?" I said, "I think you are doing great. I am really happy
for you." He said, "No, what do **YOU** think about wrestling?" "You
mean me? Actually getting in the ring and wrestling?" "Yes!" "What
are you talking about?" I asked. "There is a wrestling company in
Charlotte, North Carolina, called Jim Crockett Promotions, and Ivan
Koloff and Don Kernodle are looking for a new partner." Ivan had
been in the business for many years, and had been very successful.
He loved the idea Don had of finding a "nephew" which would
only further his career. I would become that nephew.

The road to success is paved with a great mentor.

I asked Animal, "Do they know I have never been in the ring or hit a ring rope?" "Yes, they know." "What do I have to do?" "Call the promoter Jim Crockett." So I did. I called Charlotte, North Carolina, and spoke with Jim Crockett. I introduced myself on the telephone. With no more than a five-minute conversation, Mr. Crockett instructed me to be in his office on June 4th with my head shaved bald. "I'll see you then," I said, and hung up the phone. I immediately called Animal back and informed him of our conversation and then thanked him for the opportunity.

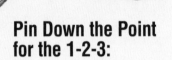

Pin Down the Point
for the 1-2-3:

1. If a guy named Animal calls, take the call.

2. To get what you want, you gotta go out and get it.

3. Serendipity is God's way of remaining anonymous.

World six-man tag-team champions, Krusher Kruschev, "Uncle" Ivan Koloff, and Nikita Koloff, Richmond Coliseum, Richmond, VA (1985).

Chapter  **8**

THE DAY AT CROCKETT'S NWA OFFICE

OPTIONS LIMITED
OPPORTUNITIES UNLIMITED

"It's not the critic who counts: not the
man who points out how the strong man
stumbles or where the doer of deeds
could have done better. The credit
belongs to the man who is actually in the
arena, whose face is marred by dust and
sweat and blood, who strives valiantly,
who errs and comes up short again and
again, because there is no effort without
error or shortcoming, but who knows the
great enthusiasms, the great devotions,
who spends himself for a worthy cause;
who, at the best, knows in the end, the
triumph of high achievement and who, at
the worst, if he fails, at least he fails while
daring greatly, so that his place shall
never be with those cold and timid souls
who knew neither victory or defeat."

-- Theodore Roosevelt

Prior to Animal's phone call, I was working as a mail courier for a private delivery company by day, and spinning the wick (that's right, a disc jockey) at a discotheque at night. My options seemed pretty limited at that point, although I had lined up a pro football tryout with the USFL. My hopes were to use it as a springboard to the NFL, thus fulfilling my childhood dream.

On the other hand, the opportunities seemed so unlimited with pro wrestling. I had watched Animal and his partner Hawk's success over the previous year; the Road Warriors had catapulted themselves to stardom virtually overnight.

Keeping your focus brings an edge to your game.

I figured I had nothing to lose by giving wrestling a shot, and if it didn't work out, I still had the football tryout.

Sometimes even when you are winning you must keep fighting.

June 4th rolled around rather quickly, and I proceeded to load up my car with every possession I owned, and the $250 I had to my name, and I headed off to a city and state to which I had never been.

I arrived in Charlotte on the morning of June 4th, 1984, walked into the offices of Mid-Atlantic Championship Wrestling, and introduced myself to Mr. Crockett. He took a look at me. Then he asked me to remove my shirt. He took another look at me. Then he asked me to remain where I was and he would be right back.

He walked down a long hallway and through a door. When he re-entered, he was with two other guys, Don Kernodle and Ivan Koloff, the NWA/WCW world tag-team champions. He introduced me to them as their new tag-team partner. They looked at me, looked at each other, looked back at me, looked back at each other, and said, "WOW! Okay."

As Winston Churchill would say, to be a success you must have a "never give up" attitude.

Ivan and Don were doing interviews that day in the office studio. Jim Crockett instructed me to accompany them during the interviews and to have my shirt off, hold Ivan's chains, stand behind them, fold my arms, not say anything, and just look mean. At this point I thought, okay, shave your head, look mean in an interview, don't say a word. Boy, this business is easy. Little did I know what I was in for.

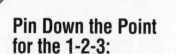

Pin Down the Point
for the 1-2-3:

1. The "critic" doesn't count. "Pay no attention to what the critics say; no statue has ever been erected to a critic." -- Jean Sibelius
"No statue has ever been erected to a critic, but of the people they have criticized, many statues have gone up." -- Glenn W. Turner

2. You can't make efforts and never expect to make errors.

3. Shaving your head is no big deal if it means being successful.

Chapter  9

GETTING AN ELEVEN-SECOND WIN UNDER YOUR BELT

"Definition of courage: grace under pressure."

-- *Ernest Hemingway, former wrestler*

At the conclusion of these interviews, Mr. Crockett informed me that next evening at Dorton Arena in Raleigh, North Carolina, they would be doing a huge four-hour television taping of the who's who of wrestling, and I was to be there and have my first match. He instructed Ivan, Don, and me to be there early so I could learn a couple things prior to getting in the ring for the television match.

But we got there late, and there wasn't really any time to get in the ring and do anything. Mr. Crockett didn't want to let me wrestle, but Ivan convinced him to give me a chance. The one thing Ivan came back and said was, "No matter what you do, don't trip on the ropes." Apparently Mr. Crockett said if I tripped on the ropes getting into the ring, I would be history.

"Okay, I can do that. Beyond not tripping, what do I do?" Don pulled me aside in the locker room and showed me some very basic things. Having the outcome predetermined, we only needed to interject a few moves to bring me to the point of the outcome. Then the outcome would take care of itself.

The arena was sold out with over fifteen thousand people. It was June, hot and sweaty, and it was lights, cameras, and action.

Nobody knew me from Adam, but the fact that I was associated with Ivan and Don brought a loud unison of boos.

At match time, we entered the ring amidst a sea of boos and a barrage of insults. The bell rang. Being a teachable student, I followed exactly what Don had instructed me to do. Eleven seconds later, I had my first victory under my belt. First victory in a wrestling match. First victory on television. And my career was launched.

For the next couple of months, I became a master student. You may not get an eleven-second win your first time out; it may take twelve seconds. The key lies in your preparation when the opportunity presents itself.

"To win a match in eleven seconds takes a lifetime of preparation."

-- *Nikita Koloff*

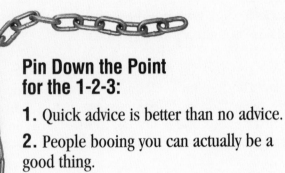

Pin Down the Point for the 1-2-3:

1. Quick advice is better than no advice.

2. People booing you can actually be a good thing.

3. Great courage can overcome greater pressure.

Always ready. Always in character.

Chapter  10

NIKITA'S SUCCESS BACKGROUND MOVES TO THE FOREGROUND.

THEY NEVER ASKED ME -- I JUST DID IT TWENTY YEARS BEFORE NIKE TOLD ME TO.

"Whatever you are, be a good one."
-- Abraham Lincoln

Don, Ivan, and I would get to the town where the next match was to be held a couple of hours early, and the three of us would work out in the ring. I was doing my "on the job training" at this time. I took to it like a duck to water. I didn't find it very difficult to learn.

I had one match each night. Ivan, as my "uncle" and mentor, would sit in the corner and watch my match. Then, when it was their turn, I would escort Don and Ivan to the ring, sit in the corner, and observe their match. I wasn't just sitting there as a prop for the show. I was sitting there as a student, to watch and learn the business.

At the conclusion of the show, and sometimes late into the night, we would discuss the things I did right, the things I did wrong, and what I needed to improve. I asked questions regarding moves they used in their match to learn the psychology of the business.

Mental focus with a controlled
intensity lead to early success.

As time went by, I saw the potential to have a successful career in
the business, and I took it upon myself to learn as much as I could.
As with everything else in my life, I wanted to become the best.
I wanted to be a world champion.

Because I knew I could.

I was willing to pay the price to be the world champion. Which, at
this point was more of a mental challenge than a physical challenge.
I had to maintain what I had attained physically, but I also had to
learn the mental aspects of the business. And to do that I watched
many of the matches every night to see what the other wrestlers
did. I figured the more I learned from watching the experienced
guys in the ring, like Ric Flair and Dusty Rhodes, the quicker I'd
advance. I was very fortunate to work early on with some of the
superstars of wrestling, like the legendary Johnny Weaver, The
Rock 'n' Roll Express (Ricky Morton and Robert Gibson), Ricky
"The Dragon" Steamboat, and others who had years of success and
experience and were willing to teach me all they knew.

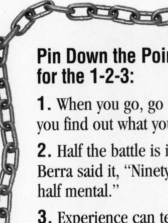

Pin Down the Point
for the 1-2-3:

1. When you go, go all out. It's the only way you find out what you're really made of.

2. Half the battle is in your mind. Or, as Yogi Berra said it, "Ninety percent of the game is half mental."

3. Experience can teach you, but execution depends on preparation.

Champions: Those who strive to become their best.

Chapter 11

THE RISE OF THE RUSSIAN NIGHTMARE

"And try to live today because today will
be yesterday when tomorrow comes."

-- William Muldoon, former wrestler

In early interviews I told "American Dream" Dusty Rhodes that I
would be his worst nightmare. And from that we decided I would
be Nikita Koloff, the Russian Nightmare. It fit perfectly with my
partner, the Russian Bear.

Many of the things we did in the ring were ideas we came up with
to generate interest from the fans as we traveled up and down the
roads. We tried to do things that would make them hate us even
more. We would come up with things to say in the interview that
would "raise their body temperature." When we would wrestle in a
military base (such as Fayetteville, North Carolina) Ivan and I would
cut a promo for that town and say, "We want to see all you soldiers
in your yellow dresses sitting in the front row."

They showed up, but not in yellow dresses. In fact, they came many
times in their fatigues, proudly waving the American flag in our faces.
And they let us know in no uncertain terms just how much they loved
and appreciated the American wrestlers, chanting in loud boisterous
voices "U-S-A, U-S-A, U-S-A." When it came time for our match, they
just wanted to kill us, or at least see our opponents kill us.

We would brainstorm different ideas as to what we would do in matches or what we would say in interviews to get people to the arena. Our success back then was based on the number of people in the seats. It was a collective effort; there were times when only one match was the main drawing card for a particular show.

But for bigger events and bigger venues, you had to have a collective effort of main event matches, because there were several matches that would get the "credit" for drawing the crowd. It became important to work well together. Not just with your opponent in the ring, but collectively with your peers on the wrestling card.

Interviews played an extremely important role in filling the arena. Don, Ivan, and I were constantly thinking of ways to develop my character, which was why I took it upon myself to study, speak, and write the Russian language. I chose not to speak English to anybody but Don and Ivan, and to do whatever it took to give me the best possible chance at becoming a world champion.

It was very important to develop a finishing move, or what is now called a signature move, that the fans could easily identify. It became obvious to me what that would be as I carried the Soviet flag around. The hammer and sickle insignia on the flag became those moves; the Soviet hammer is now called a choke slam, and the Soviet sickle is now called a clothesline. I still have people comment how it looked like I took guys' heads off, and of course, in some cases I might have (figuratively, not literally).

It also meant going to the gym six or seven days a week for a couple of hours at a time. I wanted to stay on the cutting edge mentally by learning the business and physically by looking like I thought the Russian Nightmare should.

> "Whatever you're trying to achieve, the words 'worked hard at it every day' have to be part of it."
>
> -- *Nikita Koloff*

Pin Down the Point
for the 1-2-3:

1. Don't just play a part, **BE** the part.

2. When you make decisions, make them based on the person you want to become, not just on who you are.

3. Develop a signature move.

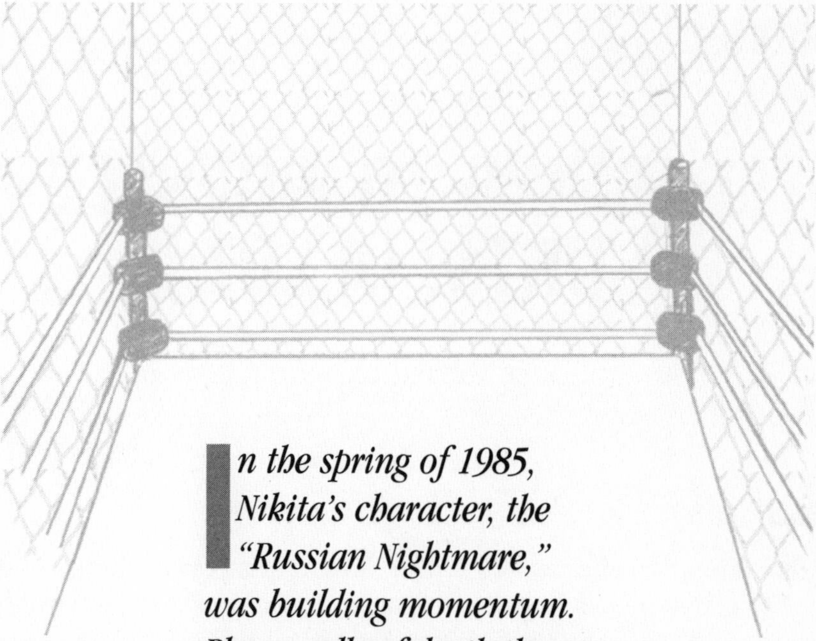

*I**n the spring of 1985,
Nikita's character, the
"Russian Nightmare,"
was building momentum.
Phone calls of death threats
for the Koloffs were
commonplace at the
wrestling office. Nikita
destroyed numerous
opponents night after
night; many times several
opponents were in the ring
at once but left bloodied
and beaten. Nikita Koloff
gradually became the
#1 most-hated villain in
professional wrestling* ● ● ●

Chapter  **12**

LEARNING TO WRESTLE HURTS. (A LOT.)

"You cannot purchase experience; you
must earn it."

-- *William Muldoon, former wrestler*

Getting injured and wrestling with pain are just part of the business,
something that we all knew in advance. In order to be successful,
it was just something you did. You didn't call in sick. There was no
such thing. If you were a main event wrestler, you were expected
to be there regardless.

In October of 1975, Ric Flair, "Mr. Wrestling" Tim Woods, Johnny
Valentine (Greg "The Hammer"'s father), Bob Bruggers (a former
Miami Dolphin), and David Crockett (Jim Crockett's brother)
boarded a small plane and headed off for a match in Wilmington,
North Carolina. The plane ran out of fuel and crashed before it
could reach the Wilmington airport.

David Crockett sustained some broken bones and minor injuries.
Tim Woods didn't break anything but did get beaten up and
battered and was fortunate compared to Flair, Brugger, and
Valentine, all of whom broke their backs. Tragically, the pilot lost
his life. Although Flair didn't wrestle that night, he recovered and
wrestled thirty more years. Brugger sustained multiple broken bones
that required permanent steel rods and pins throughout his back
and never wrestled again. Johnny Valentine was paralyzed from the
waist down and never wrestled again. Tim Woods, on the other

hand, did wrestle that night because "the show must go on," as the promoter would say. As the main event, Tim was expected to be there. Ric Flair is on record as saying, "Tim Woods saved the wrestling business."

If you were promoted in the main event match, and people expected to see you there, you had to be there. If you weren't, it tremendously affected the outcome of the event for that evening. And it would affect the outcome of future events, in the form of ticket sales. The fans would think "If they weren't here last time, how do I know they will be here this time?" So it was critical to be there; missing a match just wasn't an option.

Our only time off was for about a week prior to Christmas, and then Christmas usually was a double shot, wrestling that afternoon and that night. Otherwise, it was a year-round sport. No off-season.

Sometimes you need to push past the pain to reach the top.

If you were a top name, there was a good possibility you would be wrestling every night. There were weekends when we would wrestle Friday night, be in Atlanta Saturday morning to film the TBS wrestling show at 8 A.M. which would air that evening at 6:05 P.M., and then wrestle Saturday afternoon, Saturday night, and Sunday afternoon and Sunday night all in different towns. It was common to have six or seven matches between all the different towns and the television tapings on a particular weekend.

For example, the promoter might schedule Richmond, Virginia, and Baltimore, Maryland, in the same night, and Ric Flair and I would be the main event matches in both towns. We would wrestle the third match in Richmond, which made the people madder than hornets that we weren't the last match. Then we would jump in

limos that took us to the plane, fly to Baltimore, and jump in limos waiting to take us to the arena. The second event would have started at 8 P.M., and Ric and I would enter the ring at midnight. We then wrestled for fifty-five minutes, after we had already wrestled for thirty-five minutes in Richmond earlier that evening.

The schedule was very rigorous, especially if you were a main event name. The promoter wanted to get the most out of you. Whining would have been detrimental to your career. What impressed the promoter more than anything was the guy who didn't whine and sucked it up. That really encouraged the promoter to use him more. The promoter knew you were

How do you handle adversity?

a team player, and he knew that you weren't going to drop the ball in the face of a challenge. You gained a lot more respect from the promoter when you did that. There were guys who whined, and because they did, they ended up being the opening match, or at best, middle of the card.

What is it you need to break free from?

Pin Down the Point
for the 1-2-3:

1. If you get knocked down, get back up with a plan about how to either make friends with your opponent or knock him down.

2. Experience costs, but it's a small price to pay in exchange for what you get. You earn your own experience.

3. To succeed, you need a daily attitude of determination and a passion about what you're doing.

••• *Wrestling promoters began to consider having Nikita wrestle the legendary Ric Flair for the world's heavyweight title. Despite Nikita's lack of experience in the ring, his tenacity and overbearing presence caused such a stir among the fans that they would on more than one occasion attack him in the ring. Each attack made Nikita stronger. He could beat three and four men at a time and finish them off with his notorious move, the Russian Sickle. The crowd booed. He was hated. And rightfully so* •••

Chapter  13

LIVING THE PART

"Everybody has their ups and downs,
so I decided to have mine between good
and great."

-- *Daniel Hoogterp*

What did it take to live the character? The three "Ds." Desire.
Dedication. Discipline. But it really was a mind-set. What I wanted
to do was protect the character I was developing. To do that I had
to be cautious in everything I did and everything I said throughout
the course of the day. If I went out in public alone, I had to be
prepared for the possibility of someone questioning me.

One time at a grocery store, I was picking out fruit, and a young
man walked up to me and spoke fluent Russian. I stood there,
not saying anything, trying to figure out how to get out of this one.
I said to him with a heavy accent, "We in America now, we speak
English." So he said, "Okay," and spoke broken English to me.
I quickly broke off the conversation and walked away.

He was an employee at the store, from Russia, and he ended up
bagging my groceries. He tried speaking to me again on my way
out of the store, to which I replied, "Da," which means yes in
Russian. He could have said my mother was a fat cow and I
wouldn't have known the difference. I just wanted to get out of
there. That was really the only verbal confrontation that I had
during the tenure of my wrestling career.

I also had wrestling fans who brought me Russian/English

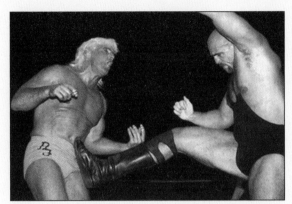

It takes courage to hang in, even when you get hit below the belt.

dictionaries to help me learn the English language so they could communicate with me. Many of the fans wanted me to speak English so badly. I had to apply the discipline I had from my earlier years on the football field and in the weight room, along with my desire to succeed, to lead the fans to believe or "buy in" to the idea that I was from Russia.

For me, the character was a 24/7 mind-set. I was always conscious of where I was, who I was with, and who I could trust (from the standpoint that if I were to speak "normal" English around them as opposed to broken English, they wouldn't run and tell somebody).

I studied enough of the Russian language to get by. I figured that Americans would never figure it out anyway. To Americans, anything I said sounded like Russian. I would put words and some phrases together here and there that I knew would throw them off. But they didn't really know what I was saying. Sometimes neither did I.

There are plenty of people who to this day still think I am Russian. With the help of the Internet and my speaking engagements, it has been a very slow process of bringing people around to the fact that

I am not really from Russia. When I retired from the business, the tough part for me was shifting from the Russian accent mind-set back to a total English-speaking mind-set. For at least two years, I really maintained that character, partly because I wanted to protect the business I was involved in, and partly because I wasn't sure how to make the transition back. I started to put less emphasis on the accent to give the impression that I was learning the English language and improving. I was trying to slowly phase it out; hoping that this way fewer people would react negatively to my speaking English.

The most difficult part was hanging around with people outside of the ring. It was hard speaking to them without the accent. Even at home, around my wife and children. I was 100 percent trying to protect the business and the character that I had built. That is what really brought my character to the level of success that it had -- the fact that I was willing to put 100 percent effort into its success.

Nowadays, I don't carry the accent. There are still a lot of people who recognize my name and face, and I hear comments like, "What happened to the accent?" I tell them it retired when I did. I find that many people still expect me to continue to maintain or live that character. Some fans tell me how disappointed they are when they find out it was just a character. They are in shock and "just can't believe" their bubble has been burst. They believed it for twenty years.

> "It's not acting the part, it's not playing the part, it's **LIVING** the part."
>
> *-- Nikita Koloff*

Nikita uses his championship belt to illustrate a point.

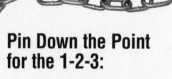

Pin Down the Point
for the 1-2-3:

1. Live your "character" for what you plan to be.

2. How are you living the three "Ds"?

3. A positive mind-set will make "down times" up and will make "up times" great.

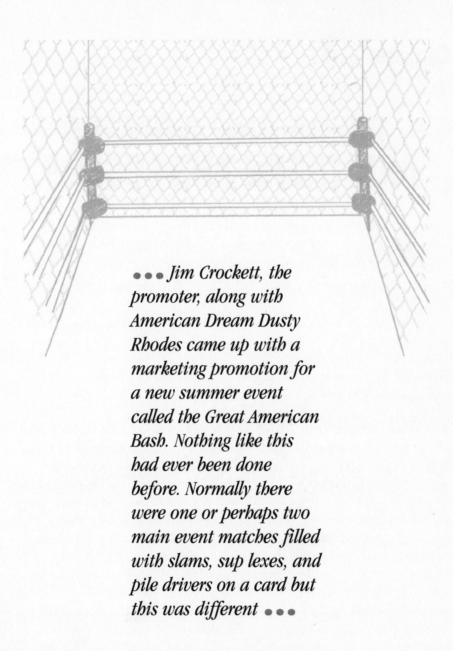

●●● *Jim Crockett, the promoter, along with American Dream Dusty Rhodes came up with a marketing promotion for a new summer event called the Great American Bash. Nothing like this had ever been done before. Normally there were one or perhaps two main event matches filled with slams, sup lexes, and pile drivers on a card but this was different* ●●●

Chapter  14

THERE ARE WINNERS AND THERE ARE LOSERS.

"Always remember: the value of time, the success of perseverance, the worth of character, the power of kindness, the influence of example, and the obligation of duty."

-- Marshall Field

Koloff: Here are some thoughts and ideas about winning and losing as they relate to life:

1. Losing a match (not a life) -- When I stepped into the squared circle, I lost some matches. However, I won a lot more than I lost. When I stepped onto the football field, I lost a few games. But again, I won more than I lost. Coach John Richmond once told me, "It's not a sin to get knocked down. It's only one if you stay down." He told me that in 1980 and I've never forgotten it. I carried it with me through the rest of my football days as well as my wrestling days and into the business world, and I'm teaching it to my children. In this wrestling match called life, you're gonna lose a few matches. You can't avoid it. It's just a part of life. The key to success is how you respond to those losses. I've been fortunate to turn my defeats into victories (i.e., what appeared to be a career-ending injury as an eighteen-year-old turned out to be motivation that led to success). What about you? In life you're faced with many adversities. Will you not accept the adversities along with the good things that happen? Losing a match in your life is not the end. It's only the beginning, if you allow it to be. I challenge you to turn your defeats into victories.

You may just be a loser. Here's how to find out: How bad do you want it? In a wrestling match, there's a winner and a loser. It's how the loser handles the loss that determines whether or not he is victorious the next time out. The same is true in life. There are winners and there are losers. So you lost the sale to your competitor. How bad do you want to make the next sale? Your desire to make the next sale will determine whether or not you experience victory or defeat. It's all up to you. If you've made it this far in this book, congratulations! You're on the road to success.

2. Inspiration from the wisdom of others -- positive or negative --
Inspiration or Exasperation. I've been blessed to surround myself with a number of individuals from whom I have gleaned many pearls of wisdom. Each time I leave them I feel inspired to achieve more. I've been around others who've left me feeling exasperated. I leave them not wanting to see them anymore. Who have you surrounded yourself with?

3. Predetermined outcomes in every phase of your life --
I am a huge believer in having balance in my life. I take my wife out on dates often. I go to lunch with my children often. I don't plan these dates on the fly. I've already predetermined when and where the date will take place and that careful planning usually results in a good outcome. I place a high level of importance on my relationships with my family and friends. I've become an avid book reader in hopes of increasing my knowledge and skills. How often do you read? I'm not talking about the sports page or the comics. I'm talking about a book that will improve your life skills. I go to the gym six days a week. I've been doing this for over thirty years. How often do you go? My family and I go to church on Sunday, we read our Bible, and we pray every day. I believe in order to be well-rounded and successful I need to develop the physical, mental, and spiritual aspects of my life. It has worked quite well.

4. Making predetermined outcomes work for you -- Discipline.
Discipline. Discipline. How much do you have? The greatest
contributor to my success has been my ability to discipline myself.
I have been fortunate to have different visions and ideas of things
I wanted to accomplish, but in order to bring it to fruition, I had
to take action. I looked at the muscle man in the magazine and
decided I wanted to look like that. I bought a weight set and started
lifting the weights. The picture in the magazine helped me
predetermine the outcome.

**5. Attitude to start, goals to continue, responsibility and
determination to win** -- I had a positive attitude that I could look
like the muscle man in the magazine. Lifting weights became an
easy way to set goals and to measure the success. I learned a long
time ago that you can't hit a target you can't see. Therefore I used
a journal to record my progress along the way. Training partners
would hold me responsible, and with their motivation, it became
easier to win. I think it's imperative to your success to have written
goals, a time limit to complete them, a vision for what you want to
accomplish, and a partner to help you along the way, be it a wife,
husband, or friend.

Gitomer: I went to my fortieth high school reunion (do not try to
do the math). The first person I ran into was Dave Lomax. A good
friend in high school and a state champion wrestler. A real nice guy.

Back then, we ate lunch together almost every day, and lunch for
Dave was always a struggle to either keep his weight or make his
weight because he wrestled at 130-something but he really weighed
140-something. The idea was that if you could lose a few pounds,
your strength would be greater in a lower weight class.

Every week Lomax struggled and every week Lomax won. I believe
in his entire high school career he only lost two matches. He was
dedicated. He was passionate. And he loved to win.

I brought my high school yearbook with me for people to re-sign. I took a look at the wrestling photo, and everyone was standing with his shoulder facing the camera and one arm behind his back to reveal their chest and arm physiques, and they were smiling -- with pride. The reason they had pride was that they were confident of who they were, they were dedicated to their excellence, they were self-disciplined to the edge, and they were winners. Many of them were champions.

Interesting to note that when one person became a champion, it seemed to raise everyone else's level of commitment because they also wanted to be champions. The whole wrestling team at Haddonfield Memorial High School took on a new challenge: See how many state champions they could breed.

At the core of their winning, at the core of their pride, was the agony of their training. Lomax always had tape around something. He was always training on weekends and after school. He didn't do as much socializing as others, but he got way more recognition. He didn't have to go out and make friends. People wanted to be his friend.

And as I looked at that yearbook picture, I saw that every guy who had wrestled as a senior in my senior year had made it to the reunion that night. It seemed as if the pride had carried through for forty years.

Here are some additional thoughts and ideas about winning and losing as they relate to life:

1. Losing a match (not a life) -- Everybody takes loss a different way. But it's the person who converts anger to determination who will ultimately end up on top. You may see Tiger Woods get angry if he misses a putt. But you will also see him for two hours after the match on the practice putting green determined not to miss it again. That is called playing on a championship level.

2. You may just be a loser -- Here's how to find out. Ask yourself this. How did it feel when you lost? Did you tell yourself you weren't good enough? Or did you tell yourself you could have or should have won? If you think you could have won, then ask yourself how badly you really want to win. That answer will determine your level of determination. Your level of commitment. Your level of passion to win the next time.

3. Getting inspiration to win from the wisdom of others --
By talking to other champions in an engaging manner (i.e., not begging or groveling for their time), you can learn what it took for them to become winners. You can learn about their wrestling matches and how they won them, or why they lost them. I'm sure you've heard the phrase, "Why reinvent the wheel?" The answer to that is, there's no reason to reinvent the wheel. There are so many champions out there that you're foolish not to befriend several of them who can provide bits of information to help piece your puzzle together.

4. Selling your story with passion -- Whether you are trying to make a big sale, trying to complete a big deal, or just asking your banker for a loan, you're telling a story. And the more passionate that process is, the more likely others will be compelled to buy from you. Passion is the intangible element that creates personal attraction. Passion is the magnet that will draw people to you and accept you. Passion is the key to motivating yourself.

5. Predetermine your outcomes in every phase of your life --
A huge part of wrestling is the preparation for the match. If you are physically fit and you are mentally fit, then it is likely that you will also be emotionally fit. And that balance makes your outcomes more predictable. If you look at the career of Nikita Koloff, you will see a person who was always ready to win. He was always fit. He was always passionate. He was always dedicated. He was always self-disciplined. And he always thought of himself as a winner. And still does. And still is. Nikita Koloff is the dictionary definition of predetermining your outcomes with preparation.

6. Making predetermined outcomes work for you --

One of the biggest problems with graduating from high school or college and making the transition to the business world is losing the self-discipline of preparation. Getting ready. Doing your homework. Studying. You know, all the things your parents had to force you to do. Now that your business card is printed, you may be out of that habit. You may also not be winning or succeeding as much as you think you should. Jeez, I wonder if there's a coincidence there? I wonder if there's a correlation between student and winner? Your ability and desire to get ready will match your success outcomes. But here's the secret: Pick something that you want to come out your way and figure out what you need to do to get ready to win in advance. Decide what your daily dose needs to be and execute the plan until you pull off the victory. Once you have one predetermined outcome tucked under your belt, buy a bigger belt. You'll need it.

6.5 There's a secret behind predetermining your outcomes.

It started when you were two years old. Your mother or father read you the book, *The Little Engine That Could*. I think I can, I think I can. That was a turning point for you if you chose to take it. And there were probably five hundred others between then and now. Chances for you to become a more positive thinker about your life and the outcomes you'll derive from it. The secret is positive thought. The formula is: Positive thought will lead to or yield positive outcome. The secret behind the secret is that no one gives you positive thought. You give it to yourself. It's a gift. It's a blessing. It costs you nothing. It's worth a fortune. Bless yourself. Forever.

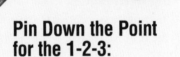

Pin Down the Point
for the 1-2-3:

1. If you aren't winning, it's because you aren't prepared to win.

2. The personal pride you store from previous winnings will drive you to your next win.

3. Winners: Attitude, responsibility, and the determination to win.

●●● *This would be a huge wrestling card of all main event matches, featuring marquee names from around the country combined with a musical concert held in a large outdoor stadium. The very first ever Great American Bash was to be held at Memorial Stadium in Charlotte, North Carolina, a venue that would hold approximately 40,000 people. Forty thousand people, all of whom wanted to see Nikita Koloff go down in defeat and up in flames* ●●●

Part

3

Staying Ready

Ever walk down the street and notice the shape that people are in? Most of them have something between a spare tire and an SUV wrapped around their gut.

The statistics on overweight people are not just staggering, they're frightening.

Staying ready is a self-discipline that will keep you on the path to success.

Sure, there are a lot of successful fat people, but what's the fun of becoming successful if you can't even fit in your pants?

Staying ready has several components. Through this part of the book, you will understand each one of them and be challenged to figure out what it takes to win the championship.

Chapter 15

MIND OVER *EVERYTHING!*

"Great spirits have always encountered
violent opposition from mediocre minds."

-- Albert Einstein

"Man's mind stretched to a new idea
never goes back to its original
dimension."

-- Oliver Wendell Holmes

"You become what you think about all
day long."

-- Earl Nightengale

The mental and psychological parts of the wrestling business
encompassed learning to control the fans in the seat. The key to the
business was for me to dictate to the fans what I wanted, not for the
fans to dictate to me what they wanted. And how I was able to do
this was to develop an ear to listen to the fans, and to have a good
working relationship with my opponent.

In a sense, the match was a dance. If you are dancing with
someone, you have to work in unity together. Then it will flow.
Dancing in the ring, if you flowed with your opponent, made a
better match. The better the match was, the better story you could
tell to the audience, and the better story you told, the more the
audience was into it. The audience never knew what kind of role
they played in the match, but it was very significant.

On a military speaking tour. Left to right: Road Warrior Animal, Hawk, an American soldier, Nikita Koloff, Larry Kerychuk, and an American soldier at the DMZ (demilitarized zone). North Korea can be seen in the background.

The more you learned the psychology of the game, the more successful you were. That's why some of the guys who were in the business for years hadn't risen; they never learned the psychology of the business. They had the physical abilities and skills to functionally have the match, but they just couldn't quite put the mental, the psychological, and the physical together.

An intangible part of the business was microphone skills. Hulk Hogan developed great microphone skills. He wasn't considered the greatest wrestler in terms of wrestling-ring skills, but his charisma in front of the camera overshadowed what he lacked in the ring. Ric Flair was the complete package. He had the physical abilities, he understood the psychology of the business, and he had great microphone skills and charisma that led him to excel past everyone.

This was the art of the business. Yes, the outcomes were predetermined, but from the opening bell up to that outcome, everything was spontaneous. It was psychology, the ability to dictate to the crowd what you wanted them to do, and too do it on the fly in the heat of the action.

In business, you might formulate a plan for a presentation, but sometimes a monkey wrench is thrown into the picture, and the best salesperson is the one who is able to change direction on the spur of the moment, without the audience knowing what he or she did. That is what made a world champion wrestler. Change directions, change thought, change ideas on the spur of the moment, without the audience knowing. This ability makes a true champion.

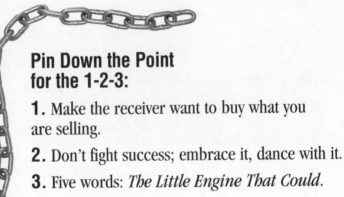

Pin Down the Point
for the 1-2-3:

1. Make the receiver want to buy what you are selling.

2. Don't fight success; embrace it, dance with it.

3. Five words: *The Little Engine That Could*.

••• *Not ever having wrestled Flair before, it was critical to come up with a creative strategy that would draw the interest of the fans. The goal was to fill the stadium with 40,000 screaming, lunatic wrestling fans. As the creative juices flowed, they decided to do a television series of video vignettes to enrage fans and cause more bad blood between the Americans and the hated Soviets. Uncle Ivan and Nikita were already the world tag-team champions, and along with Don Kernodle, the world six-man tag-team champions. The most obvious storyline was for Nikita to win the world heavyweight championship and take all the gold back to Moscow because that's what the Kremlin ordered •••*

Chapter 16

BODY FIT OR FAT?
BRAIN FIT OR FAT?
HINT: THEY'RE RELATED.

"People do not lack strength; they
lack will."

-- Victor Hugo

"A house is no home unless it contains
food and fire for the mind as well as for
the body."

-- Margaret Fuller

If you eat a steak and mashed potatoes and garlic bread with butter
and creamed spinach and a salad and more bread and butter and a
bottle of wine and cheesecake with sauce on it and coffee and an
after-dinner drink, you're not going to be able to do anything other
than go home and fall asleep in front of the television (if you can
make it that far). If by some chance you have work to do the next
day, your brain will not be fit. You'll wake up with a headache or
cotton-mouth or an upset stomach, or all three. Your productivity
will drop. Your ability to think creatively will be diminished and
you'll be on the path to fat and unproductive. Body or brain, take
your choice.

If you're looking for success, the key will lie in your ability to
moderate your intake on days when you are not working and

Nikita speaks all over the world. Here he is in Johannesburg, South Africa.

minimize, if not eliminate, bad body intake the day before you have to be mentally alert.

Gitomer: I've been giving speeches for eleven years on the road. I've given more than 1,000 speeches in front of the some of the largest companies in the world. I have never, nor will I ever, have a social glass of wine or beer the evening before an event. I'm not saying that my brain is always fit. Nor am I saying that my body is always fit. But I am saying that when it counts, the only person I can count on to be my best is me. If I cheat, the only person I'm cheating on is myself. And if my performance is not up to par, the person who will know it most is me.

At this moment you may be thinking "Yeah, but I can get away with it." Yeah? So can I. What's your point? The place where you and I differ, or may differ, is that I am always striving to be my best. And the only reason that I can strive to be my best is that I am fully ready to be my best. When I go back to my room at night, or when I go to my office at night, my mind is clear to think and create. And that's how your mind needs to be in order to be ready to succeed.

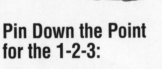

Pin Down the Point
for the 1-2-3:

1. For some reason I don't understand, physical balance leads to mental clarity.

2. If you eat too much, you'll get fat.

3. Look around, almost everyone is either a bit too fat or way too fat. You can be ahead of almost everyone if you just get more fit.

••• Ivan made the inaugural announcement on television, and aptly named the plan, "The Road to Moscow." Ivan made it very clear that the road to Moscow would be paved with gold and the blood of Ric Flair. Ivan came on the interview set and demanded a contract from Crockett Promotions for Nikita to wrestle Ric Flair for the world's heavyweight title at the Great American Bash. The announcer, an arrogant David Crockett, said they didn't know who was going to wrestle Ric Flair because there were many formidable opponents more qualified than Nikita •••

Chapter  17

THE INSPIRATION TO BECOME A STUDENT

"To become different from what we are, we must have some awareness of what we are."

-- Bruce Lee

"Formal education will earn you a living. Self-education will earn you a fortune."

-- Jim Rohn

As with every business, I faced adversity from other guys in my business. In your business, perhaps, you will face adversity from your competitor, or in my case, an opponent. It may not only be from an outside source that you face adversity; it may be internally, with someone else on the sales force.

I did. I did in the form of jealousy from the other wrestlers who had been in the business longer than I had. Sometimes much longer. Sometimes years longer. And they hadn't received the break that I was receiving, after only being there for a short time. I was getting the push, getting the camera time, moving right into main event status, as opposed to having to start with the opening match or middle of the card. All because I was prepared. Had I not been, I would not have excelled at the opportunity I was given. But I was prepared, and it allowed me to achieve the level of success that I did.

Nikita reaches out to a new generation (2003).

The other guys didn't go the extra mile or take the extra time in the gym. I would go home many nights and study wrestling films. I would try to learn the psychology and mental aspects through tapes too. And I had Ivan and Don there to answer my questions.

I was willing and eager to learn new things ... forever. I made a decision to become a lifetime student (when the day comes that I think I know everything, that's the day I hope He takes me home).

I had become a student, teachable, coachable, and willing to listen to the masters, Ivan and Don. I was willing to learn without my ego getting in the way, or having too much pride. One of the things that helped me with success was that I didn't let success go to my head. I was able to maintain a certain level of humility that, as I look back, I see enabled me to excel at a rapid rate.

Throughout my career, I never considered myself a student greater than the teacher. I never got to the point where I thought I knew it all. I was always willing to learn something new, if there was something new to learn. Because of the discipline, dedication, and commitment I made to the business, the first major highlight of my career took place in July of 1985, thirteen months after my inaugural match, wrestling Ric Flair for the heavyweight title in front of 35,000 people. This night was instrumental for me from the standpoint that I was able to see a payoff for the effort that I had put in for the thirteen months prior. A payoff, literally and figuratively.

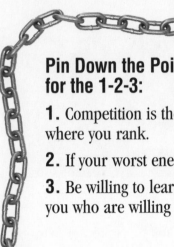

Pin Down the Point
for the 1-2-3:

1. Competition is the part of life that shows you where you rank.

2. If your worst enemy is yourself, make peace.

3. Be willing to learn from people better than you who are willing to teach.

*••• But Ivan didn't care.
It only irritated him to
hear David Crockett say
Nikita wasn't qualified.
Ivan protested, "We are
the world tag-team
champions and the world
six-man champions,
and the Kremlin has
ordered Nikita to become
the world heavyweight
champion." But David
Crockett didn't care.
Crockett Promotions
wasn't under the orders
from the Kremlin •••*

Chapter  18

HOME SCHOOLING AFTER YOU GRADUATE -- COMBINING KNOWLEDGE AND TALENT TO BUILD PERSONAL CHARACTER

Talent may get you there -- but character
will sustain you.

-- Nikita Koloff

"The manner in which you perform your
daily tasks builds and reveals your
personal character."

-- Spark Matsunaga

"I'll take care of my character; my
reputation will take care of itself."

-- Dwight L. Moody

I had the privilege of homeschooling my own children for two
years. Even though I was teaching them and they were learning,
I was learning at the same time. I've made a personal commitment
to myself to forever be a student.

South Korean fans learn what it means to be ready (2003).

I graduated from college with honors and felt I had learned a lot while I was there. I've used the talents and gifts that I've been given to succeed in many ways, both on and off the playing field. I've had the privilege of being around people from all walks of life and all different levels of success. I've been around winners. And I've been around losers. I've been around those who had limited talents, but because they had character, became winners. I've been around those who had tremendous talent and no character and became losers.

Talent can take you to the top, but character is the only thing that will keep you there. This has been very evident in recent years as we've seen corporate executives fall.

Character is doing the right thing when no one else is around. You're out of town and you don't know anyone. You are in the hotel gift shop by yourself. You see a magazine that you've determined is no longer appropriate for you to read. Hey, no one's around and no one can see you. Or can they? You decide not to thumb through it and you hold on to your integrity. That's character.

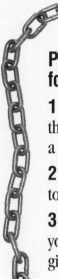

Pin Down the Point
for the 1-2-3:

1. The day you finally graduate from school is the day you must dedicate yourself to remaining a student.

2. What you learn in school pales by comparison to what you learn in the world.

3. Character is not just what you have, it's who you are. And here's the best part: Character is a gift you give yourself.

●●● *During one interview Ivan made it known that Nikita was in strict, serious training to prepare for his match with Ric Flair even though no contract had been signed. In fact, he had a training segment he wanted to show. The announcer, David Crockett, turned and said, "Ladies and gentlemen, as much as I don't want to show this video, I have to show it because they have bought the airtime. We have no choice but to show it." Uncle Ivan ordered him to roll tape* ●●●

Chapter 19

HOW TO GET CROWD REACTION -- MY ACCENT ACHIEVED BUY-IN TO MY RUSSIAN WRESTLING CHARACTER

"A successful individual typically sets his
goal somewhat, but not too much, above
his last achievement. In this way he
steadily raises his level of aspiration."

-- *Kurt Lewin*

"The reason they boo is that they want
to cheer."

-- *Anonymous*

Why did so many people buy in to my character? Why did the
crowd react when I entered the arena or the ring? Why did they
boo me when I was a "bad guy"? Why did they cheer me when
I was a "good guy"? How is it that I was rated the number-one-
most-hated guy in wrestling and then I made the transition to one of
the most popular guys in wrestling? (When I teamed up with The
American Dream, Dusty Rhodes, and we became the Super Powers,
all was forgiven.) The lesson here is simple: It was because of my

photo by Greg Russell

Nikita tells a church congregation about his Russian wrestler character.

will to succeed, making the necessary sacrifices, and the commitment to become one of the best at what I did.

It's been said all things are possible to those who believe. I got crowd reaction, and they bought into me because I believed. And because I believed they believed. What are you doing to get crowd reaction? You must believe in what you're doing for the other person to buy in. Whether it's a family member, a friend, a co-worker, or anyone else, they must believe that you believe before they'll believe. Are you believable? Are you sincere? Is it from the heart?

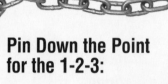

Pin Down the Point
for the 1-2-3:

1. Learn to speak the language.

2. The crowd will love you or hate you based on what you say and what you do. You determine whether it's a boo or a cheer.

3. If you believe in yourself, and you give enough to others, then you'll receive what the world has in store for you. If you don't like what you're receiving, it means you're short on believing and way short on giving.

●●● *Nikita's training took place in a dark, dingy dungeon. A single bulb hung down as the sole source of light in this room with black walls, red lockers, the Soviet flag, lots of weights, and a heavy bag with a picture of Ric Flair taped to it. The first week of this special footage, Nikita was bench-pressing 500 pounds for reps, while Ivan stood over him and barked commands. He shouted, "Come on, Nikita, one more. We must defeat this Ric Flair. You must win the heavyweight title." As the video concluded, David Crockett said, "Very impressive, Ivan, but the decision has not been made as to who will wrestle Ric Flair." This only fueled Ivan's anger further* ●●●

Chapter 20

HOLDING IT TOGETHER WHEN YOU HAVE TO

"When in a contest you are so tired you cannot go another second, think how tired your opponent must be."

-- *William Muldoon, former wrestler*

"If not me, who? If not now, when?"

-- *Rabbi Hillel*

One Friday night, I was wrestling Ric Flair in Norfolk, Virginia, with a one-hour time limit. The match ended in a draw. We wrestled the next night in Richmond, Virginia, for almost an hour. And at 5 A.M. on Sunday morning, I woke up with the most excruciating pain in my lower back that I had ever felt. I literally had to roll out of bed, crawl on my hands and knees to the living room, attempt to find a comfortable position, and try to stretch out my lower back. Anything that would bring relief to the pain. I called the wrestlers' orthopedic surgeon, and he told me to meet him at a walk-in clinic. I had to have someone drive me to the clinic while I lay in the backseat of my car, like a dog with his legs up in the air.

I got to the clinic, and the specialist wasn't there. I saw the doctor on call and told him I couldn't move. The doc said I just had a pinched nerve and told me I would be okay, and I could go ahead and leave. On the way out to my car, my specialist walked in and told me to come back in. He could tell from my expression that I was not all right. I went back in and after the exam, I was told that my lower sacroiliac was tremendously out of place, and his first recommendation was to see a chiropractor as soon as possible and see if he could get it back into alignment.

In the meantime, I was scheduled to wrestle in the main event that afternoon in Charlotte against Ric Flair, and again that evening at the Omni in Atlanta, also against Ric Flair. Both shows were a sellout. And here I was at 10 A.M. on Sunday morning, trying to figure out how to walk. I tried to explain this to the orthopedic specialist. The best he could do for me that day was to give me a prescription for muscle relaxers and show me some exercises to do

The struggle my leave you bloodied and hurt, but how you respond to adversity is key to your success.

over the next three hours before bell time at the coliseum. I would do whatever I had to do to get in the ring that night and wrestle. I tried as best I could to time taking the muscle relaxer to kick in as I was getting into the ring.

Getting dressed was a major ordeal; trying to put socks on my feet, putting on my tights, and getting stretched out were among the most painful things I had ever experienced. It ranked right up there with the broken legs. But I did it.

I walked to the ring with a sellout crowd watching and without any of the fans knowing the pain I was experiencing. Once the adrenaline got going, and the muscle relaxers kicked in, I was okay for the next forty-five minutes of the match. However, thirty minutes after the match, I could hardly move. Then I had to get to the airport, get on an airplane, fly to Atlanta, and do the whole thing again. With just as much or more pain as I had had earlier that night. I could barely walk to the ring, but the athlete in me pulled me through. After I wrestled for fifty more minutes in the Omni and finished that match, I had to try to convince the promoter to give me a couple of days off.

I got two days off and went to the chiropractor as suggested. I flew back to Charlotte that Sunday night, and I went first thing Monday morning, Monday afternoon, Tuesday morning, and Tuesday afternoon, and Wednesday morning. I received adjustments and acupuncture. By Wednesday night, I was "good as new," back in the ring, and wrestling full-speed again, pain-free. Once again, the show must go on.

In the book of Job, we read about a man who faced what seemed like insurmountable odds. He lost all ten of his children in a tragic accident, and he was robbed by thieves of all of his wealth. His servants informed him one by one of the misfortunes. He contracted a disease that covered him with boils from the tip of his head to his feet, his friends turned their backs on him, and even his own wife asked him why he didn't just die so he wouldn't have to experience any more misery. His response to his wife was staggering. He said, "should we accept the good things in life but not the adversity?" And in the end, he held on to his integrity.

How do you handle adversity? Perhaps you are going through adversity right now. Maybe you have a strained relationship with a spouse, a child, a boss, or fellow employee. Are you handling it with integrity?

Maybe you're battling a disease of your own, and the doctor hasn't given you much hope. Or you've lost a loved one due to an illness or an accident. Again I ask, are you handling the adversity with integrity?

It's been said, if you faint in the day of adversity, your strength is

Getting the audience pumped up in Eugene, OR (2003).

small. We all face trials, tribulation, and adversity in life. There's no getting around it. I've certainly had my share, inside and outside the squared circle. The question is, how do we handle it?

During the 2003–2004 season, Brett Favre, all-pro starting quarterback for the Green Bay Packers lost his coach, best friend, and father to a sudden heart attack the day before his team's critical game on Monday Night Football. A loss would put his team out of the playoff picture. How did he handle the adversity? After consulting with coaches, friends, and family, he chose to play, rose to the occasion, and had one of the best games of his pro career.

I'm not trying to minimize the pain, suffering, or adversity you are going through. What I am doing is challenging you to rise to the occasion. It's in the face of adversity, when we hold together what we have, that true champions are forged. Courage, confidence, and integrity. It's what makes Brett Favre an all-pro, me a world champion, and what will ultimately make you a world champion.

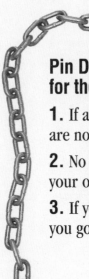

Pin Down the Point
for the 1-2-3:

1. If anyone **EVER** tells you that chiropractors are no good, have them call me personally.

2. No pain, no gain. Pain sucks, but it reveals your other characteristics.

3. If you want to be a success, when you gotta, you gotta.

●●● *Ivan came out
again the next week
and demanded a
contract be signed for
Nikita to wrestle Ric
Flair. Crockett, true to
his arrogant nature,
called Ivan and Nikita
dirty, low-down, no-
good Communists. You
could see the anger
and fury all over their
faces when they heard
those words* ●●●

Chapter 21

IT WAS, IS, AND ALWAYS WILL BE TOTAL ATTITUDE.

> "I'm a big believer in starting with high standards and raising them. We make progress only when we push ourselves to the highest level. If we don't progress, we backslide into bad habits, laziness, and poor attitude."
>
> *-- Dan Gable, former wrestler*

They say attitude is everything. I'm convinced they are right. Adopt a "do-it-now" attitude because **NOW** is the time to succeed. My attitude began in the ghetto.

Ghetto Attitude -- I was determined I could be more. I had two choices. One, I could wallow in self-pity over the circumstances I was born into. Or two, I could use my circumstances as motivation to succeed in life. Which route do you think I chose?

Leg Recovery Attitude -- Leg shattered, life shattered, or so I thought at first. Thanks to my coach's comment, I got an attitude. "I'll show him and everyone else I can come back," I thought. And I did.

Wrestling Attitude -- If I'm gonna do this, if I'm gonna wrestle, I'm going to become the best. A world champion. I'll do what it takes to learn the language, speak the language, write the language, and learn the wrestling business. And I did.

Money Attitude -- I didn't have a lot growing up so I wasn't about to squander it when I did have it. I've been labeled frugal, along with many other colorful words. I've come to realize it's not how much money you make, but what you do with the money you make. You can live the lifestyle of a millionaire without being a millionaire if you're smart with your money. I've also implemented a very important principle: He who sows sparingly also reaps sparingly, and he who sows bountifully also reaps bountifully. The farmer plants more than one seed in order to reap a harvest. How many seeds do you sow?

Mental Attitude -- I've become a book reader. I average three to four books a month. With knowledge comes understanding and wisdom. None of which I have nearly enough of. That's why I have the attitude that I need to learn more. I will forever be a student. The day I believe I know it all will be the day I hope someone puts me in my place and brings me back to reality.

Health Attitude -- In my wrestling days I was 285 pounds, had a 34-inch waist, and sported only 8 percent body fat. I no longer display that physique, but I do work out six days a week. I don't see the use for a sound mind if my body is made of mush. A healthy body supports an active and creative mind.

Spiritual Attitude -- I was successful but unfulfilled. Not until October of 1993 when I gave my life to Christ did I understand true balance in life. I searched for all the answers in all the wrong places to fill the hole. Then, I became whole.

Success Attitude -- Success begins as an attitude before it becomes an actuality. Success in one area of life tends to foster success in other areas. The degree of success you achieve depends on the amount of desire you possess. One common mistake unsuccessful people make is that they try to *find* time instead of *making* time. Don't try to *find* time, *make* time.

Pin Down the Point
for the 1-2-3:

1. Attitude is everything. But you gotta study it to get it.

2. To rise above the rest takes a blend of attitudes: mental, physical, and spiritual. This combination will lead you down the yellow brick road. (That's the road your bank is located on.)

3. Tomorrow is not the time. Now is the time.

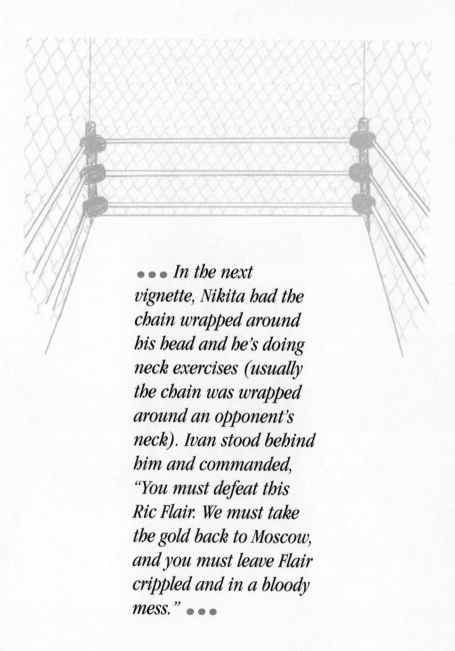

●●● In the next vignette, Nikita had the chain wrapped around his head and he's doing neck exercises (usually the chain was wrapped around an opponent's neck). Ivan stood behind him and commanded, "You must defeat this Ric Flair. We must take the gold back to Moscow, and you must leave Flair crippled and in a bloody mess." ●●●

Part

4

Are You
Ready?

READING WILL HELP YOU UNDERSTAND, BUT YOU LEARN BY DOING.

As you meander through life's experiences, you learn lessons. Some are hard, some are soft. All are good.

Business is a blend of everything you understand and everything you've learned. And the interesting part is, there's a lesson every day as long as you are willing to learn.

As you go through this section, you'll see lessons that Nikita learned as a businessperson. You will also see how his wrestling career impacted those lessons.

Chapter 22

OWNING A GYM WAS MY AHA!

(PEOPLE JOINED, BUT NEVER CAME.)

> "All worthwhile men have good thoughts, good ideas, and good intentions -- but precious few of them ever translate those into action."
>
> *-- John Hancock Field*

> "If you want to succeed in business, son, you gotta fail a few times."
>
> *-- Max Gitomer*

Three years prior to leaving the wrestling business, I was thinking ahead to what I might do when I retired. The thought was to capitalize on my name from all the exposure I had received from television. One option I took advantage of was to open up a health club, which we called Nikita's Fortress of Fitness. We eventually expanded to a second and a third health club.

This was my first venture in partnering with someone. I learned a lot about partnerships, especially that you really need to do some deep thought and soul-searching if you are considering partnering with someone in a business. I have seen businesses and partnerships ruin the best of friendships. I have seen it because I have experienced it firsthand. It is very critical that all of you are on the same page. If there are any disagreements in the business, my recommendation

photo by Greg Russell

Nikita signs autographs after a lecture.

would be to iron those out prior to signing the paperwork to be as certain as you can that there is no miscommunication.

We brought a third person into the picture, and instead of that third person becoming an asset, he became a wedge between me and my original partner. I dissolved the partnership, and I wasn't excited about having any future partnerships. Later, my wife and I decided to open our own health club.

When it comes to business, I have found that knowledge is good, and necessary, but that sometimes who you know can be better. You don't have to know everything, but if you can surround yourself with people who have answers that you don't, at times that can be much more beneficial than you expending the energy and time to gain the knowledge.

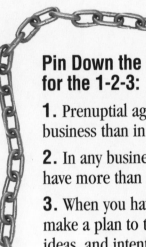

Pin Down the Point
for the 1-2-3:

1. Prenuptial agreements are more important in business than in marriage.

2. In any business partnership, make sure you have more than half.

3. When you have a good thought, you must also make a plan to transfer your good thoughts, ideas, and intentions into actions.

●●● *Nikita stood there doing dumbbell curls while the camera focused on his rock-solid 20-inch-plus biceps. You could see the blood flowing through veins as big as garden hoses. Ivan was smacking Nikita on the head shouting, "More. More. Harder. Harder, Nikita." Ivan stepped up the intensity each week, still trying to get that contract signed for his nephew Nikita* ●●●

Chapter 23

OWNING MY OWN
EVERYTHING!

"The greatest success comes not from
money, power, or fame, but from a
happy marriage, a happy family, and
a happy home."

-- Robert Elkington Wood

Sole ownership is exciting and fun, but for many people, the business
ends up owning them. There has to be a balance to have a fulfilled
life. The gyms ended up owning my wife and me. I constantly had
to be there or things would get dropped and left unfinished.

The old cliché of "good help is hard to find" is often true. Being
the decision-maker, I found it was sometimes tough making the
decisions as the sole owner, but nevertheless, the decisions still had
to be made. Whether it was hiring or firing or buying products, a
decision was still necessary. Because of these things, I am a much
better person today than I was prior to owning those clubs.

Eventually my wife and I sold the gym and moved into investment
and multilevel-marketing. This move gave us the freedom to set our
own hours, which was great for our family. Financially, it opened
the door for unlimited opportunity and success.

My definition of true success is: noseprints on the window. Huh?
If I pull into the driveway and my children are in the window
looking for me, I consider myself successful beyond measure.

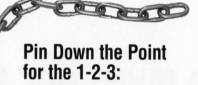

Pin Down the Point for the 1-2-3:

1. Material possessions don't bring you happiness, but they sure are fun.

2. If you're going to buy material things, make sure you can afford them.

3. Not making a decision will not resolve the issue.

●●● *Nikita pounded the heavy bag that had the picture of Flair taped to it, using his finishing move, the Russian Sickle. Sweat and perspiration poured off his body. He grunted with a heavy Russian accent, repeating over and over, "I destroy Ric Fair. I destroy Ric Fair. I destroy Ric Fair." Nikita looked into the camera with a cold, steely eyed stare and said, "Ric Fair, I going destroy you." And the camera faded to black* ●●●

Chapter 24

MAKING YOUR OWN SUCCESS

"If it is to be, it's up to me."

-- Lou Thesz, former wrestler

People have different ideas, conceptions, and *mis*conceptions of multilevel-marketing (MLM). However, for myself I have nothing but respect for those who attempt it and for the industry itself. I regard it as one of the best entrepreneurial opportunities going today without the high risk of owning your own business. Example: for my health club, I pulled $50,000 out of my own pocket in addition to loans and leases with no guarantee of success. Learned a lot, didn't lose money, but did not get rich either.

With MLM, I learned for a nominal fee that the potential is genuinely unlimited. Keep in mind there are good companies and bad ones out there, as with any business. With one company, I invested $249 and yielded a return of six figures. That doesn't include the profit I made from the stock. And just like purchasing a car, a person has to find the right vehicle in the arena that fits them. I did not get as wealthy as some of the stories tell. However, the education I acquired, the business knowledge that I gained, and the speaking opportunities that were presented to me far outweigh any kind of monetary gain I could ever receive. And I would be remiss if I didn't mention the people I met from all walks of life. It's a real education just meeting people, period. Some of my dearest friends are a result of my involvement in this industry. I've made lifetime friendships with John and Suzie Joyce, John and Denise Outlaw (their real names), Linda Kedy, and countless others. How do you put a price on friendships?

The MLM industry, and my association with educational and motivational speakers, opened up a whole new realm of possibilities via seminars, books, and tapes.

Ty Boyd, Jim Rohn, and Jeffrey Gitomer, as well as other speakers, were very influential in my current ability to speak in front of crowds that have, to date, exceeded 43,000.

Because of MLM, I was introduced to this whole world, and it was instrumental in helping me reach where I am today through my speaking skills. There is no way I could put a price tag on that.

If you have made an attempt at one of these types of businesses and it didn't work, my hope is that you don't fault the industry. If you went to a fast-food restaurant and had a bad experience, that doesn't mean all fast-food chain restaurants are like that. Same with MLM. They aren't all bad; it just means you had a bad experience with that specific company. I personally have had success with some of those companies, but I have also failed with some of those companies. I used the failures as motivation to succeed with other companies. The number-one biggest lesson that is missed with MLM is not success or failure, but who you become and what you learn along the way.

If you've ever played the stock market, then you know there is obviously a much higher risk in the investment arena. However, there are levels of risk that correspond to your return on investment. The higher the risk, the higher the potential return; the lower the risk, the lower the potential return. It's all relative, and it's all risky. I have tried as high-risk as investing in the movie industry. I rolled the dice and failed. I regard real estate as a low-risk investment. I have had tremendous success.

I also made an investment in the restaurant industry. Fortunately for me, I was involved more in the investment end than the operational end with restaurant chains that had successful track records.

The younger you are, the higher and greater risk you can take because you have a greater number of years to recover if your investments fail. The older you are, the recommendation is to lower the risk, even though the return is not as great. The reason being that you don't have as many years left to recover financially from something high-risk that may not succeed.

In business, it's not only IQ that matters, it's not necessarily great transactions that matter. There are a lot of other factors that can make the difference between success and failure. When I broke into wrestling in 1984, I informed Don and Ivan that I would be retired and out of the wrestling business by the time I was thirty-five. After two weeks of arguing with them and insisting I would retire, I finally reached an agreement and said I would be in a *position* to retire from the business if I chose to. I beat my goal by two years.

The tragedy in the professional sports arena (not limited to wrestlers) is that most athletes have no clue how to manage their money. People in general have absolutely zero idea on how to manage money. Which is why many of my colleagues are still wrestling to this day. Coupled with the fact that they claim "wrestling is all I know how to do." Sad but true.

Most people find themselves at the age of fifty-five with barely $200 in their savings account. They may have worked hard along the way, but unfortunately, have nothing, per se, to show for it. The bank owns their house, the bank owns their car, and the credit card company owns their furniture.

There is a solution. There is an answer. It is called money management. It's called a financial advisor. They are out there, available, and not costly. You may think you can't afford one. But the reality is, you can't afford *not* to have one if you have a genuine desire to live a comfortable, secured retirement. I was fortunate to befriend a gentleman by the name of Bill Staten who was very instrumental in coaching me in the dos and don'ts of stock investments. If you don't have a financial advisor, find one.

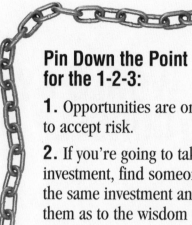

Pin Down the Point for the 1-2-3:

1. Opportunities are only limited by your capacity to accept risk.

2. If you're going to take a risk and make an investment, find someone who has already made the same investment and did well. Consult with them as to the wisdom of your investment.

3. Many people say no risk, no return. I say, no risk, no nothing. If you never take risks, you'll never achieve your potential.

●●● *The wrestling office was flooded with letters from fans who were concerned for Nature Boy Ric Flair. Unanimously they begged the promoter not to allow a match between Nikita and Ric Flair. The fans were afraid Nikita would seriously injure Flair and put him out of wrestling* ●●●

Chapter 25

CHANGE THE WORLD BY CHANGING YOURSELF

"It only takes one person to change your life -- you."

-- Ruth Casey

"Each of us finds in others the very faults others find in us."

-- Nikita Koloff

Koloff: A gravestone in England says, "I set out to change the world but quickly realized I couldn't. So I decided to change my nation but realized I couldn't do that either. So I decided to change my city. When that didn't happen I thought, I'll just change my family. But that didn't happen either. And then it hit me. Why don't I just change myself? And when I did, it changed my family, my city, my nation, and my world."

Oh, how hard we work on trying to change others. If we would only take the time to look at the man in the mirror. So how do we change ourselves? Consistency over time is the key. An apple a day keeps the doctor away. Should that be true, then wouldn't it make sense to eat that apple every day if it would indeed prevent sickness?

Wouldn't it also make sense that if you read a few pages a day of a good book or listened for a few minutes to a good audiotape, that it would lead to improved life skills? Here's the secret: Success isn't instant, it's consistent.

How hard is it to get ready? Mentally believe you can, physically prepare yourself, and spiritually seek His guidance. Personal desire determines your own fate. When I was in the ghetto, I had two choices: success or failure. It's easy to make excuses for failure. If you are going to be successful, you must shift from excuse thinking to creative thinking. Don't say, "I'll never get that job." Instead say, "What do I need to do to get that job?" Get creative. Stop making excuses.

Get ready first. When I was given the wrestling opportunity, I was ready. Success came one day later.

Gitomer: Are you ready, or are you a time-wasting grumbler?

What does it take to become a success? I listened to those words in 1972 from the great Glenn W. Turner. He answered the question in a thirty-minute talk called "Challenge to America." I watched that film two hundred times. It's now on VHS. I still watch the film.

It was the classic challenge to change the way you think so that you can change the way you act, so that you can change your outcomes. The positive thought is behind the positive outcome. Once you make the decision to think in the positive, all of your fate-levels are set several notches higher. And those fate-levels are self-determined.

No one comes to your door in the morning to give you a better lease on life. No one comes to your door in the morning to give you an excuse for why you did or didn't. No one comes to your door in the morning to tell you how to think, positive or negative. You determine that.

And so I embarked on my quest for success utilizing the vehicle of positive attitude. And through a ton of failures along the way (and two tons of successes), whenever I fell down, my attitude was the cushion. And it is that consistency of positive thought that has driven my fate-level and my success outcome.

I wake up in the morning knowing it will be a great day. And from there I call upon last night's preparation and the morning's final thoughts to go out and conquer my world.

Sure, my world is better now. Sure, my world is easier for me now. Sure, my world has less monetary pressure on it than ever before -- because my thoughts, actions, determination, and self-discipline are different now than when I was flat broke. Every day, rich or poor, I woke up, and I wake up, ready to win. Every speech I give, I'm ready. Every sales pitch I'm in, I'm ready. Every opportunity I serendipitously come upon, I'm ready.

And I owe all of that readiness to learning from the wisdom of others. In the days before computers, my dad always had a yellow legal pad in his briefcase. I could hardly read his writing. But whenever we went into a meeting together, he always referred to the notes on his legal pad, and he won way more often than he lost. He was ready. "Do your homework, son," he would say. I always responded, "Yeah," but I never really understood it until he was gone. And I reflected on that wisdom, and reflected on my own successes, and I realized that every major one was the result of me doing my homework. Of me getting ready. And so I pass the words of wisdom on to you for old time's sake: Do your homework.

Pin Down the Point for the 1-2-3:

1. Others can inspire you, but you gotta do the work.

2. Your two choices are either I think I can or I think I can't.

3. Do your homework.

●●● *Ric Flair and Nikita still had not had any dialogue, confrontation, or contact. Would Nikita wrestle Ric Flair for the heavyweight title? Would Ivan and Nikita take all the gold back to Moscow? Fans were convinced that Nikita would indeed win if he and Flair wrestled. In the meantime, a big match was announced for the card each week. And it was still yet to be determined who would be Flair's opponent* ●●●

Chapter  **26**

LOVE WHAT YOU DO, NOT THE MONEY FROM WHAT YOU DO.

"The first test of a really great man is his humility."

-- John Ruskin

"To be successful, the first thing to do is fall in love with your work."

-- Sister Mary Lauretta

Gitomer: Gee, maybe there is a little more to life than just my bank account.

You've heard the expression before, the love of money is the root of all evil. Many of the wealthiest people have died miserable and lonely deaths. Howard Hughes is one name that comes to mind.

Find something you can get passionate about, and work at it until you succeed. I have found through conversation that the majority of people take a job, not because they enjoy it or are passionate about it, but because of the income they might make. Eighty-five percent of people today hate their jobs. I would say based on the number of people I meet that that percentage is fairly accurate.

Success is born of passion and excitement. Do you love what you do?

My formula for success is: Search for something you are passionate about. Find something that excites you. Find something that when you wake up in the morning, you are eager to go after. Despite the salary, your passion and love for what you do will ultimately far outweigh any lack of monetary gain.

One day, I was watching an interview with an all-pro wide receiver for the Minnesota Vikings who was having an illustrious career. He was asked, "Why do you still play the game?" His response was, "I don't play for the money, I play for love of the game." And his actions on the field made it obvious that he enjoyed and was passionate about what he was doing. Are you?

There has to be more to making money than making money.

"The key is not how much money you make, but what you do with the money you make."

-- Nikita Koloff

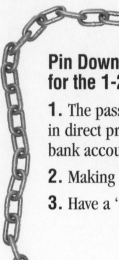

Pin Down the Point
for the 1-2-3:

1. The passion you have for your job will be in direct proportion to the size of your bank account.

2. Making money is easy, keeping money is hard.

3. Have a "love" of the game. Your game.

●●● *A few weeks before the event, Ivan and Nikita were on the interview set with David Crockett in Shelby, North Carolina. Upset that a contract had not been signed for nephew Nikita, Ivan got into a heated discussion with David Crockett, while Nikita paced back and forth. Crockett made another of his derogatory comments. Nikita had had enough so he turned and charged David Crockett and hit him with the Russian sickle. Crockett flew six feet off the ground, parallel to the floor, and hit the floor with a loud thump. He lay flat on his back and was comatose. The play-by-play guys were stunned. They didn't know what to say or do. The paramedics ran up on the stage. The fans went crazy. They didn't know if his neck was broken. They had never seen anything like this before. It caught everyone by surprise (especially David Crockett)* ●●●

Chapter 27

YOU HAVE BEEN IN A WRESTLING MATCH ALL YOUR LIFE -- WRESTLING WITH YOURSELF.

"It's kind of like wrestling a gorilla. You don't stop when you get tired. You stop when the gorilla gets tired."

-- Anonymous

Wrestle with your time.

Wrestle with your priorities.

Wrestle with your money.

Wrestle with your family.

Wrestle with your balance.

Wrestle with your boss.

Wrestle with your customers.

Wrestle with your guilt.

Wrestle with your time.

Wrestle with your time.

Wrestle with your time.

Wrestling is the best way to describe how everyone deals with life's daily situations. You can probably think of one hundred times that you have wrestled with something within the last seven days. Making a decision, dealing with a loved one, a situation at work, a budget, your finances -- I could go on for another twenty pages.

Rather, what I would like to point out is that the outcome is in your hands. Even though you may not think it is. You may think, for example, that because you have no money, you cannot pay the bill. When in fact you can:

1. Get another job.

2. Get a different job that pays more money.

3. Not spend as much (the hardest one of all).

4. Plan for the next occurrence by making a budget.

5. Call the person you can't pay and arrange a payment that you will be able to make;

and on and on.

You can probably think of ten more answers. The lesson is, most people spend more time wrestling with the problem than wrestling with the solution. The object is to pin down the answer. The object is to win this time, or sacrifice victory so that you can be better prepared to win next time, but either way to feel good about it, either for a victory or a lesson learned. Never a defeat. The only defeat you will ever incur is when you quit wrestling. I believe in the squared circle -- they call it a submission hold.

It never ceases to amaze me that one man's stress is another man's victory simply by the way they choose to view the situation and act on the solution. The ones who concentrate on the problem always have stress. The ones who concentrate on the solution always have greater self-determination and an expectation of a positive outcome. Make certain that if you wrestle with yourself, you always win your match.

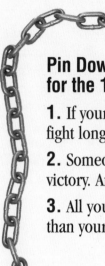

Pin Down the Point
for the 1-2-3:

1. If your opponent is stronger, they'll fight longer.

2. Someone else's stress can become your victory. And vice versa.

3. All you need to win is to be 1 percent better than your opponent.

••• *Crockett and Flair had become good friends after surviving a plane crash together in Wilmington, North Carolina in 1975. Knowing this, Uncle Ivan felt that if Nikita attacked a close friend of Flair's, he would be forced to sign the contract. Later in the show, Ivan and Nikita were in the ring preparing for a match. Flair came out to the staging area and began to yell insults at Uncle Ivan. Ivan threw them back. Flair couldn't contain himself anymore and jumped off the stage. As he did, the arena erupted into a roar* •••

Chapter  28

IS YOUR RECIPE LEAN AND MEAN, OR FAST FOOD FAT?

"You must never despair; our situation has been compromising before, and it changed for the better; so I trust it will again. If difficulties arise, we must put forth new exertion and proportion our efforts to the exigencies of the times."

-- George Washington, former wrestler

Before you read this, go back and re-read "Body Fit or Fat? Brain Fit or Fat?" in Part 3.

Here's the recipe for getting ready on your own.

The first thing you do is measure the brain fat. How much of your twenty-four-hour brain time is productive? Probably less than the amount of unproductive. Here are five things you can do to invest your time more wisely:

1. Read in the morning for fifteen minutes; pick something about positive attitude or success.

2. Call one person each day who knows more than you do and try to build a better friendship or association with him or her.

3. In your car, listen to positive, educational CDs that might give you an idea or two.

4. Always be reading a book on creativity.

5. Begin the self-discipline of writing -- writing your thoughts, writing your goals, writing your visions. Start a journal or continuing document that you will be able to use as a guideline and a reflection of where you were, where you are, and where you want to be.

The second thing to do is measure the amount of healthy food against the amount of unhealthy food that you take in. Here are five things you can do to make your food intake somewhat more healthy. Keep in mind, this is being written by a person who has violated many commandments of food intake.

1. In the morning, eat water-based fruit to start your day, such as an apple or a pear.

2. Drink at least sixty-four ounces of water sporadically throughout the day. (Double that if you want to learn where every restroom is around the world.)

3. Substitute one caffeine-free for one caffeinated drink each day, i.e., fruit juice versus soda.

4. Reduce the amount of sugar in your diet, especially as the day progresses.

5. Eat more protein and less carbohydrates, no matter what any vegetarian tells you.

Bonus fact: Any time you justify fat intake by preceding it with the word "only" it will lead to undesired pounds that are nearly impossible to shed without the hardest workouts of your life.

And third, measure your exercise time versus your sofa time. There's a new disease known as the furniture disease that's very prevalent in men. It's when your chest falls to your drawers. It is more commonly known as beer belly. It seems as though America, without regard to gender, is expanding both in population and size of butt.

Here are five things you can do that will increase your blood flow and decrease your chance for heart attack and butt attack.

1. Spend less than thirty minutes a day on any piece of furniture other than your office chair and your bed at night except when you are actually sleeping (or ... you know).

2. Add extra walking steps wherever possible. Park farther away in the parking lot. Take the stairs instead of the elevator.

3. Commit three hours a week to physical exercise, broken into three one-hour segments. I don't care what you do as long as you do something. Something is better than nothing.

4. Add jogging to your regimen. Start with a mile. Work up to four miles twice a week.

5. Play some active sport. Doesn't matter what it is, as long as you do it once a week. And for those of you trying to justify golf as an active sport, let's just say, at best it's semi-active. If you're driving in a cart, it's inactive. If you're drinking after the match, it's reactive.

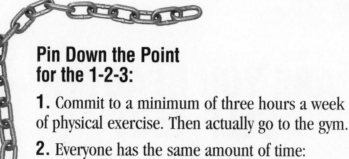

Pin Down the Point for the 1-2-3:

1. Commit to a minimum of three hours a week of physical exercise. Then actually go to the gym.

2. Everyone has the same amount of time: twenty-four hours a day. The difference between success and failure is how you choose to invest it. Everyone has the same stomach. The difference in size is the type of food you put into it.

3. Your car can be a university of self-improvement and new knowledge, or a vast wasteland. It all depends on what you listen to as you drive.

••• *Flair rolled into the ring and took off his jacket. Never breaking character, Nikita stood there with his stoic Russian look. Flair charged and hit Nikita on the side of the head with an open hand. Not fazing Nikita, Flair tackled him next, and they rolled around the ring as the fans went absolutely crazy. This was the one and only time Flair and Nikita had any contact with each other. As they exchanged punches and blows, other wrestlers jumped in the ring. The Rock 'n' Roll Express, the Road Warriors, Dusty Rhodes, Barry Windham, Arn Anderson, Tully Blanchard, and others had to tear the two apart. The crowd was still going absolutely ballistic. They were at a pitched frenzy. And the show went off the air* •••

Chapter 

ARE YOU READY?: SELF-TEST

"Never mistake motion for action."

-- Ernest Hemingway, former wrestler

Hopefully by now we've given you some real food for thought.
More than that, we hope we've given you some meat to chew on.

One thing that I've learned to do when reading a book or listening
to a speaker is to chew on the meat and spit out the bones.
Not everything I read or hear applies to me. Or necessarily interests
me. But I always attempt to pull a nugget or two that I can use to
my benefit.

We've talked about getting ready, being ready, and staying ready,
and now the question is, are **YOU** ready? Are you ready to take
the following self-evaluation and see how you measure up? Your
honesty will determine your future. Take a look at the list that
follows and write down how much time you spend on each activity.
Your answers may surprise you.

WORK ETHIC–SELF-DISCIPLINE SELF-ASSESSMENT

The wealthy and the poor have this in common:
Twenty-four hours in a day.

Weekday		**Weekend**	
Sleep	_____	Productive work	_____
On the road	_____	Writing	_____
Television	_____	Thinking	_____
Eating	_____	Entertainment	_____
Exercise	_____	Improving expertise	_____
Education	_____	Television	_____

How did you do? Sleep is important, but not twelve hours or half a day. The majority of people have to commute to and from work. How do you spend that time? Music is okay, news is okay, maybe, but not really. Have you ever thought about turning your car into a university? What do I mean? You have a cassette player or CD player in your car, right? Ever thought about buying a motivational tape or CD? Most books are now available on tape or CD. Are you in sales? Then pick up *The Sales Bible* (by Jeffrey Gitomer). Why not turn this time into productive time?

My guess is that what you've been listening to is not helping to improve your position in life. The Good Book says there's a time for everything. A time for music and a time for learning. Why not use some of this time in your car for learning? How much time do you spend in front of the tube, boob? If we lived in Old Testament times, two-thirds of America would be stoned to death for gluttony.

I'm convinced a balanced diet along with exercise is a necessity for a successful life. How many seminars are you attending? I'm a big believer in improving life skills. In order to do that, that I made the decision to attend numerous seminars over the years to acquire knowledge and wisdom from others.

Weekends bring your week into balance. Where do you spend the most time? Entertainment and relaxation are important to a balanced life, but weekends also provide a tremendous opportunity to think and plan your future. How much time do you invest in improving your chosen field of endeavor? Have you ever done any writing? Writing improves your thinking. Thinking improves your planning. Planning improves your productivity. Productivity improves your future.

I spend my Sundays in church. I find that the more wisdom I gain, the more productive I become. My philosophy has become that something is better than nothing. Moderation is the key. Some exercise is better than none. Some learning tapes are better than none. Some seminars are better than none. Some thinking is better than none. Some planning is better than none. And some church is better than none.

I now live according to the "slight-edge principle." Never heard of it? Here it is: If you eat a salad today and I eat a Quarter Pounder with cheese today, the salad may not improve your health today and the Quarter Pounder with cheese may not affect my health today, but compounded over time, the law of averages says it will. I'll end up with clogged arteries, and you'll live to be a hundred.

If you read ten pages of a good book today and I read the comic strips, you may not dramatically improve your life skills today, I may (or may not, probably won't) improve my humor, but again the law of averages says that compounded over time, your level of education and success should surpass mine.

My decision to eat a Quarter Pounder with cheese or read the comics every day is what's called a simple error in judgment. Your decision to read ten pages of a good book and eat a salad every day is what I call a simple discipline. So the slight-edge principle says simple disciplines repeated over time will get you to where you want to go.

The flip side is that simple errors in judgment repeated over time will keep you where you are. The difference between success and failure is the choice between a simple error in judgment and a simple discipline practiced every day.

Pin Down the Point for the 1-2-3:

1. Not everything you read, see, or hear is positive. There's an old song with the title, "Accentuate the Positive." One of the keys to success is not letting "negative" get in your way.

2. Start every day with at least fifteen minutes of positive-information reading. This will set your mind on "positive." It's one of the secrets of success that almost no one uses to its full potential.

3. Simple self-disciplines repeated over time will lead to success. Small errors in judgment repeated over time (ten cigarettes a day, one cheeseburger a day, three beers a day) will lead to failure.

●●● *The next week the announcement was made. It would be Nikita Koloff, the Russian Nightmare, against Nature Boy Ric Flair, for the world's heavyweight title. David Crockett stood in a neck brace while he reluctantly made the announcement. Knowing what it felt like to take the Russian sickle, he had a genuine fear for his friend of what the destructive, merciless, powerful Nikita Koloff could do* ●●●

Part

5

Wearing
the Belt

THE FEELING OF SUCCESS

When you beat a champion in the ring, you have won the match and you get a belt, a championship belt, as proof of your victory. That belt is not just a symbol of the championship; it's also a symbol of personal pride. Champions carry it with them -- when they are in an interview they drape it over their shoulder, when they enter the ring they're always wearing it.

That same feeling must be transferred to your endeavors in order for you to maintain the feeling of success so that you can continue to add to it. When you have the most sales, you get a trophy or a plaque for best salesman of the month, maybe even best salesman of the year. That plaque or that trophy is displayed with pride.

When you go into someone's office, you often see diplomas, awards, photographs, and trophies. All of these are symbols of success. They may be displayed for fifty years. And each day, whether on purpose or subliminally, the recipient (hopefully you) sees them. If you look at your past success every day, it will inspire you to future success. Whatever your "belt" is, wear it with pride every day.

Chapter 30

WAS IT REAL?

"Undertake something that is difficult; it
will do you good. Unless you try to do
something beyond what you've already
mastered, you'll never grow."

-- Ronald E. Osborne

Gitomer: If you've ever watched pro wrestling, in your mind you
know it's "fake." But sometimes it looks pretty real. When you
look at the wrestlers, most of them are in phenomenal condition.
What you don't see are the hours and hours and hours of
conditioning that they went through in order to qualify for entry
into the squared circle.

Even though the outcomes are predetermined, what they're doing
inside the ring is as real as real can be.

Koloff: Sometimes it was unreal. People ask me all the time, was
wrestling real? My answer to their question is, "It's all entertainment.
But guys **REALLY** get hurt." Entertainment? Yes. Real? Yes. Real
injuries, real aches, real pain, real road trips, real airports, real
hotels, and real tired. I once wrestled seven matches in a 52-hour
period of time covering six cities and four states. Real? You bet.
Tired? You bet.

In 1986, I wrestled 454 matches in 365 days. You do the math.
Sometimes it was unreal. The travel, the injuries, the demanding
schedule, and the politics of the wrestling business (because it is
a business) made it as real as anything you've done.

Gitomer: In the end, it's not about real or fake, it's not about real or unreal, it's not about real or surreal -- it's about the individual, his preparation, his dedication, and his ability to execute (sometimes under pressure, sometimes in pain, and sometimes in front of 25,000 people).

Your ability to prepare for your success is in direct proportion to the success that you will achieve. It seems so obvious, yet so few people are really willing to prepare.

Look at Nikita Koloff's picture as a champion. That boy was ready. Lean, mean wrestling machine. He was hated, he was loved, and he was good. Darn good.

The lesson of Nikita, and the lesson you can take from Nikita, is that he never wavered in his commitment to be the best that he could be. He lived his part, he paid his dues, and he cashed his checks.

photo by Greg Russell

Nikita says, "You try it if you don't think wrestling's real."

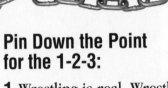

Pin Down the Point for the 1-2-3:

1.Wrestling is real. Wrestling is unreal. Wrestling is surreal. Wrestling is anything you want it to be. Same in life.

2. The more you wrestle, the better you become at wrestling. The same formula applies to any facet of business or life.

3. Make your own reality.

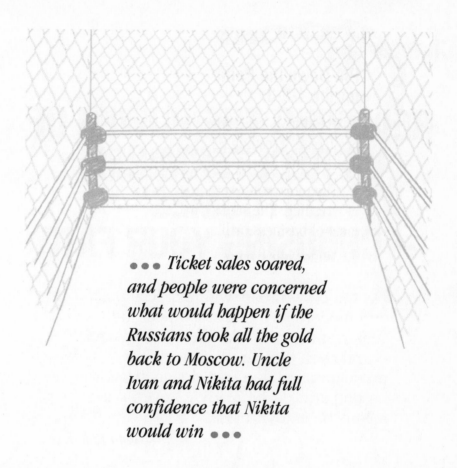

••• *Ticket sales soared, and people were concerned what would happen if the Russians took all the gold back to Moscow. Uncle Ivan and Nikita had full confidence that Nikita would win* •••

Chapter 31

REALIZING THE POWER OF "PREDETERMINED OUTCOMES" -- CHOOSING YOUR FATE

"As the crowd roars with expectation, two modern-day gladiators meet in the center of the ring (aka the squared circle) -- and even though the outcome is predetermined, the participants have to be prepared ... be ready ... even if it means be ready to lose!"

-- Nikita Koloff

"Most people are not willing to do the hard work it takes to make success easy."

-- Jeffrey Gitomer

Can you predetermine your outcome? I did it before I knew it would lead me to success. And I'm passing that wisdom along to you so that you can achieve the same thing.

How did I become a 285-pound behemoth sporting a 34-inch waist and 8 percent body fat? Did it just happen? I don't think so. As I said earlier, as a sixth grader, I picked up an Ironman magazine, flipped through page after page of muscle-bound men, and envisioned myself looking like one of those guys. It was that original vision that enabled me to predetermine that outcome.

I realized I couldn't just look at the magazine and become like that. I had to take action. I had to get in the gym. I had to lift the weights. I had to dedicate myself. And because I did, I accomplished the goal that I had set at an early age.

When I started watching the NFL, I had another dream -- that one day I would play in the NFL. But again, I realized I couldn't just watch the game on television and wait for the Minnesota Vikings to call me when I grew up and tell me they were ready for me to join their team. If I was going to play in the NFL, I had to learn the game. I had to join a team. And I wasn't content just being part of the team. I wanted to be in the starting lineup. I wanted to be catching touchdown passes. I wanted to be sacking the quarterback.

Because of hard work and determination, this dream became more of a reality when the NFL scouts showed up on my college campus and put me through a battery of NFL tests. Eventually, I lined up a pro football tryout at the same time the wrestling opportunity came about. I opted for wrestling.

When I broke into professional wrestling, I wasn't content just to be another wrestler. I decided that if I was going to do this, I was going to be a world champion. I wanted to be the best. That's why I went to the gym every day for years.

Wearing the Belt

Through hard work and determination, I became a world champion many times over. When I moved into the business world, I applied the same principles I had learned in the sports arena. Hard work, determination, goal setting, and a vision for success were all key elements leading to my personal success.

No matter what stage of life you find yourself in, what your age is, what your race is, or what your gender is, it's never too late to start. The history books are full of people who succeeded at all stages of life.

Colonel Sanders of KFC didn't become a success until his late sixties. I have a friend named Jack Countryman who's seventy-four years old and still firing on all cylinders. In fact, everyone wonders when he's going to slow down. He and his wife Marsha have built the world's largest devotional-book company.

By applying the principle of "predetermined outcomes," you can predetermine your outcomes, create your own success, and live the lifestyle you dream about.

I challenge you to invest more time dreaming.

Pin Down the Point for the 1-2-3:

1. There is no way that I can jump out of these pages and get you to do the hard work in advance of your success. But if I did jump out of these pages, many of you would be sitting in a bar or in front of a television, and that's not part of the formula. You can't just "look at magazines," you have to go after what you want from them.

2. When you dream, you envision. The more you dream, the clearer your vision becomes. There's a two-word secret to turn dreams into realities: hard work.

3. The easiest way to implement the pre-determined outcome formula is to divide your desired achievements into small daily amounts. The "daily dose" is the rocket ship. Your achievement actions are the fuel.

••• *Ivan bragged, "We will walk into the stadium that evening, win the heavyweight title, and the Kremlin will have a big parade and festivities in Red Square. There will be a huge celebration in Moscow. Nikita will go down in the annals of Soviet history as a wrestling legend and there's nothing that you stinking Americans can do about it* •••*"*

Chapter  32

MENTORS AND ASSOCIATIONS
ONLINE METHODOLOGY
FIVE TRUSTED ADVISORS/MENTORS

"Associate yourself with men of good
quality if you esteem your own
reputation; for 'tis better to be alone
than in bad company."

-- *George Washington, former wrestler*

Koloff: There are certain laws and principles in the universe that
you can't change. The law of gravity says if I throw you up in the
air, you come down. You can't change that.

There's another law that is called the "law of association." The law
of association says you'll become like the five people you hang
around the most. If you took their income, totaled it, and divided by
five, you'll find your income to be about the same or within a few
thousand dollars. So in order to increase your net worth, you must
associate yourself with people more successful than yourself.

If you are hanging around people who drink, do drugs, and cuss,
and you don't do these things, it's only a matter of time before you
will. If you want to change your outcome and your outlook, you
have to break away. Yes, it is painful to leave a friend behind, but
sometimes that experience will make you a better person in the
future. It's the law of association. Another way this has been said is,

"Birds of a feather flock together." If you don't currently have mentors, I encourage you to seek them out. One of the best ways to gain more knowledge and wisdom is to surround yourself with those who have more.

A world-renowned speaker by the name of Jim Rohn said his mentor told him to set a goal of becoming a millionaire. Jim asked the reason why. His mentor said, "It's not about attaining the million dollars. It's who you'll become along the way." I have learned that you cannot place a value on personal development. Even more valuable is to take the knowledge, understanding, and wisdom you learn and pass it on to someone else. You will not be able to measure the value of this reward. There is no greater feeling than to see a pupil, be it your child, a friend, or a business associate, become more successful because you took the time to teach, train, and mentor them.

My first encounter with a real father figure came into play in the seventh grade. I joined a football team, and the head coach's name was Bill Burke. Bill was a big, barrel-chested, macho guy. I was a little seventh grader and had never had a male role model. I just gravitated to him, and he took me under his wing. He would take me to the sporting goods store and buy me football equipment, and he became my first mentor.

Two years later, in the ninth grade, I met my second father figure/ mentor. He was a teacher at my school and happened to be a professional bodybuilder. His name was Gerry McFarland. Not only was he a health teacher and a body builder, he was also a gymnastics coach.

I spent as much time around him as possible. Whether it was during school, after school, in the evenings, on weekends, or going over to his house whenever possible, I just wanted to be around him no matter what. For the next several years, he became the driving force in my life. He personally trained me in the weight room for football. This was when my dream of playing in the NFL grew stronger.

As my skills developed, the dream became bigger and more of a reality. In all the years I was around him, I never remember him ever giving me a negative remark. Everything was always positive and encouraging.

During my freshman year of college, I was reunited with Bill Burke. He was on staff at the college I attended and in fact, was instrumental in my selection of that college. He and the head coach, Irv Nerdahl, were two great motivating factors in my continuing dream of playing in the NFL. Their years of experience in football and their encouragement after I broke my leg were priceless.

The next mentor that came into my life was my next coach, Dave Skrien. Coach Skrien had had great college and professional careers in the Canadian Football League, both as a player and a coach. In fact, in 1963, his team won the Canadian Grey Cup (their version of the Super Bowl). His knowledge, experience, and insigh were influential in my ongoing drive to play in the NFL.

The next coach to impact my life was John Richmond, my offensive line coach. Although Coach Richmond taught me many things, the one thing that stands out in my mind was, "It's not a sin to get knocked down, it's only one to stay down. So get up and get back in the game." Not only did this benefit me on the football field, but I have also taken that philosophy and adapted it to life. Through all the twists, turns, trials, and tribulations life has brought, it has helped keep me focused.

The last influential coach in my life was the head coach Ross Fortier. Coach Fortier believed in my abilities when I sometimes did not. He scouted me as a freshman in college and knew all about the broken leg, yet he was willing to take a chance on me and gave me a scholarship. I was determined not to let him down. On those days when he sensed I was feeling dejected, he always had an encouraging word. And though he may or may not have realized it at the time, it was those encouraging words that drove me to succeed on the football field and transfer that success into everyday life.

I've been very fortunate to have so many good mentors. I continue to be blessed today. Terence Rose has mentored me the last nine years, my co-author has been influential in my success, and others continue to cross my path. They are out there for you as well. But only if you look for them. They won't knock on your door looking for you, but be confident that they will cross your path.

> "Mentors are the guideposts on the road to success."
>
> *-- Jeffrey Gitomer*

Gitomer: Need help succeeding? Consider a mentor. Mentors play a major role in the life of a person trying to succeed.

What is a mentor anyway? Mentors are role models for the type of person you want to become. Someone you admire for the amount of wealth they've gained, or who rose to be the best in their field. A person you respect who can give you wisdom and guidance without prejudice. Someone who inspires you to greater achievement. Someone who provides a guiding light with words that stick with you over the years.

What do mentors give? Wisdom in nuggets. Gold that you remember and use to smooth the path (or find the path) to success. They provide inspiration and guidance when you need it most.

How can mentors help you? With the value of their experience. With the wisdom gained from their successes and failures. With practical advice that often flies in the face of the emotional frenzy of the present moment. With ideas and concepts that go beyond your present vision.

Where do you find mentors? -- At the top! If you're seeking help, get it from those who have been through the battle and won.

Why do they do it? Why do mentors take pleasure in helping you? They may be at a point in their careers where they're ready to "give back." Often your mentors were helped by *their* mentors, and they are returning the favor to the world. They want to help -- it's how you receive it that will determine whether the relationship flourishes.

Who are your mentors? If the answer is "I don't know, or I don't have one," the next 500 words can change your life. If you have one or more, here is a user's guide to maximize the benefit of, and challenge your use of, one of life's most valuable resources.

How do you get a mentor? Never say, "Will you be my mentor?" Earn the privilege, be of value, deserve it. Work hard, show promise, have a hard-work ethic, not a hard-luck story.

What do you say to (share with) mentors? What kind of help do you ask for? Share your goals. Ask their advice, their opinions. Share your triumphs, ask to hear about theirs. Share your defeats, but don't moan about them; tell them what happened and ask for advice. Tell them what you intend to do -- then do it.

How do you keep a mentor for years and years? Bring value to the relationship. Here's a list of guidelines that will nurture a mentoring relationship:

- Use them wisely -- don't overuse or abuse your privilege.

- Don't ask your mentors for money. It will prejudice their response, and you will lose their objectivity.

- They take pride in your growth. They enjoy helping you -- **BUT** -- you must thank and acknowledge them at every opportunity. That's their inspiration to continue.

- Approach potential mentors with care and respect. Go slow.

Personal Note: Mentors' wisdom has played a major role in my growth and success. I had five mentors, including my dad. Three are still alive. Their wisdom has been a guiding light, spiritual lift, wake-up call, and cold slap in the face when I needed it most. Sometimes it hurts to hear the right answer.

Here are a few examples of mentors' pearls that have helped me --

- (Responding to my perceived problems)
  Anything ten grand wouldn't cure?
  If it's something money can cure, you
  have no problems.

- Hard work makes luck!

- Success is never found or earned from nine
  to five.

- You're running here to make five grand,
  running there to make ten grand -- wanna
  make a million? Stand still!

- (Said to me by my best friend about my dad)
  You know what I hate about your old man --
  he's never wrong.

- Become your own Santa Claus.

- Keep your antennas up at all times.

Boom. Words of impact. Some of these self-evident truths were spoken to me twenty years ago and are still fresh in my mind today. That's the impact a mentor can have on your direction.

I owe more to my mentors than can be expressed in writing. They know it too -- I've told them. More important, I've shown them by adopting their wisdom and philosophies, and putting their advice into action.

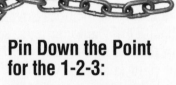

Pin Down the Point for the 1-2-3:

1. Success Challenge: Make a short list of people (possible mentors) you believe can impact your career.

2. Find a way to get to know them. Find a way to get them to know you. Find a way to get the impact of *their* success to have an impact on *your* success.

3. I hope you do.

●●● *Nikita continued practicing to sharpen and hone his skills for the big match. He knew he would leave his opponents bloodied, brutally beaten, and oftentimes, to the screaming fans' dismay, hanging over the ropes by his Russian chain after the 1-2-3. The fans intensified their hatred towards Nikita. Not a night went by that they didn't shake their fists, scream, and throw things at him. This only encouraged him more and more* ●●●

Chapter

SUCCESS IN
A BRUTAL WORLD

"When the going gets too tough for
everyone else, it's just right for the
Nature Boy."

-- *"Nature Boy" Buddy Rogers, former wrestler*

One of the motivating factors, either on the field or in the arena,
was the rush of adrenaline as I heard the cheers of the fans or the
boos of the fans. If I was competing as the "bad guy," the louder
the boos, the more frequent the heckling, the more it confirmed that
I was doing my job.

This was also why I decided to learn, speak, and write the Russian
language. I wanted to be the most convincing I could possibly be
because that would give me the greatest success. I would give it
an all-out effort.

Would it have been easier to go to the arena, play the role, and
then leave the arena, the role, and the character behind? Yes. Did
it take much more dedication, work, and discipline to carry the
character with me 24/7 for twelve years (which includes several
years after my retirement)? Yes. Was it worth it? Yes. Why? Because
it accelerated my level of success in wrestling, and it catapulted the
longevity of my success in the business and beyond. Could I have
continued the career another ten to fifteen years? Yes. Why didn't I?
It was my goal to retire and walk away as a champ on top of the
business in people's minds, as opposed to a washed-up, has-been

about whom people would ask, "When is he going to retire? Doesn't he realize how old he is?" Was I able to close that chapter in my life? Yes. Was I able to maintain the character and continue being successful? Yes. Do I use it as a platform to this day? Yes. Is it beneficial? Yes. Does it still draw them in? Yes. Am I able to make a difference in other people's lives? Yes. Do I count it a privilege and an honor? Emphatically *yes*.

No one ever said it would be easy. It's a dog-eat-dog world out there or, to put it another way, a real rat race. But there's good news: You can win without becoming a rat.

"If your name is "Nature Boy," you'd better be able to win a fight."

-- *Nikita Koloff*

Pin Down the Point
for the 1-2-3:

1. No one said it would be easy.

2. You always have to be prepared to fight for what you believe is true, for what you want, for what you love, and sometimes for who you love.

3. Seek excellence, not perfection.

••• Over 35,000 screaming maniac fans were in attendance at the Great American Bash. It was truly a history-making event. Many who have become legends in the business were part of the show that night. Most of the fans were anxiously awaiting the main event match between the world champion, Nature Boy Ric Flair, and the challenger, the Russian Nightmare Nikita Koloff. As part of the agreement in signing the contract for the world's heavyweight title, Flair insisted upon a stipulation that David Crockett be the special referee. Believing David Crockett wouldn't be impartial, Ivan countered with a stipulation of his own. He would sit in the corner of nephew Nikita to make certain Crockett called a fair match •••

Chapter 34

DO-IT-YOURSELF SUCCESS. IT'S NOT A KIT YOU CAN BUY -- IT'S A BUTT YOU CAN KICK. START KICKING WHEN YOU WAKE UP IN THE MORNING.

"There was never a horse that couldn't be rode; there was never a rider that couldn't be throwed."

-- *sign in the Oklahoma State University wrestling room*

Koloff: I don't ever want to get to the point where I think I know it all. I personally want to remain coachable, teachable, and continue to gain wisdom and understanding.

As I do that, I am not doing it to hoard it for myself, either. I want to give that information to my children, grandchildren, and anyone I come in contact with, in the hope that what I have to say will be a benefit to the listener. Always remember: Be quick to listen, slow to speak, and slow to anger.

Even at a very young age, it was a pet peeve of mine to see athletes hang around too long in any sport, whether it was for the pay-day or the ego. I decided that when I made it, I would walk away on top of the business or as a champion. When I broke into the business, my goal was to retire by thirty-five. I beat my goal by two years and officially retired just before my thirty-fourth birthday. But I continued to portray the character for several more years.

When I retired from wrestling, several factors contributed to my leaving. I had gotten married and had had children. As a husband and a father, it became increasingly difficult to travel and leave my family. In 1986, I had 454 matches, drove 2,500 miles in a car each week, and had one-million-plus frequent flier miles. When I was single, I didn't care if I slept in a hotel or in my apartment. But upon getting married, family played a critical role in my retiring.

Injuries also played a part in my retiring. Thankfully, I had no career-ending injuries, but nonetheless, they played a part.

And politics played a role. Believe it or not, there are politics in wrestling. I took a sabbatical from wrestling during the same period of time that Ted Turner was buying our company, Jim Crockett Promotions. Turner eventually changed the name of the federation from the National Wrestling Alliance (NWA) to World Championship Wrestling (WCW).

My personal reasons became their personal reasons, but not in a favorable way. They didn't understand how my personal relationships could get in the way of their business. They were shocked that wrestling wasn't the first priority in my life. Instead, I chose to put my family first. I eventually did go back, but I was not looked upon with the same "favor" as prior to my departure.

Bill Watts was brought into World Championship Wrestling (WCW) to run it when Ted Turner took over. He was a former wrestler and a former promoter of his own federation. He pulled me aside one night after he had been there for a few days; I had only been back with the company about seven weeks.

Bill said, "Nikita, you haven't been paid."

I said, "I know."

"They owe you a lot of money."

I said, "I know, Bill, but I figure Ted Turner is good for it. I have a handshake and verbal agreement with him, they are working on the contract, and they are finalizing it, and I am not worried about getting paid."

Bill said, "I would have liked to have more guys like you in my territory! I will see that you get your money and that the contract gets done."

I said, "That's fine." And I continued, "Bill, I need to tell you something. This isn't a slam on any of my wrestling peers. You are the new boss coming in and you need to understand where I am coming from."

The reason I set the record straight was because in those days Bill had the reputation of being a verbally abusive tyrant. I had seen that a couple times in the past and had thought to myself, I could never work for him because if he ever talked to me that way, I couldn't put up with it. I told Bill that the reason I had come back was as a favor to someone. I said, "I have a college education, and I have business investments and a health club back home. So in essence what I am saying is, I don't need this job. But if I can bring value to the company, and be a benefit to you as the boss, I will be more than happy to do that."

Bill said, "I appreciate that. I understand where you're coming from. Thank you very much."

I believe that conversation gained me the respect from him that he really didn't have for most of the other guys.

I will never forget a night in Philadelphia when I could hear him two floors down, chewing out guys behind closed doors, and I thought to myself, "I'd be walking." I only had one altercation where he attempted to fine me $1,000 for something. I felt the punishment was unjust and I immediately confronted him on it. He brought all the concerned parties together, and he recanted his decision as the truth came out.

Moral of the story: Stand up for what you believe, speak up for what you believe, and be willing to fight for what you believe.

Ultimately the person responsible for my success was the man in the mirror (me), just as the person responsible for your success is the person you see in the mirror (you). It starts when you wake up in the morning. Don't just roll over -- get out of bed. None of my successes could have happened if I hadn't kicked my own butt each morning. I've always been a winner in my own eyes. Are you a winner in yours? Don't let others take advantage and run roughshod over you. There's a critic in every crowd. Be your own toughest critic.

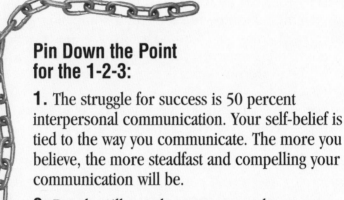

Pin Down the Point
for the 1-2-3:

1. The struggle for success is 50 percent interpersonal communication. Your self-belief is tied to the way you communicate. The more you believe, the more steadfast and compelling your communication will be.

2. People will not always treat you the way you treat them. That should not change the way you treat people.

3. Life ain't fair.

●●● *Following a concert by David Allen Coe, the bell rang for the matches to begin. Slams, sup lexes, pile drivers, cow bells, steel chains, and many other sounds filled the night air at this outdoor venue. One by one the preliminary matches ended, leading to the excitement and anticipation of the main event* ●●●

Chapter 35

THE HABIT OF HABIT -- GETTING IN THE SUCCESS HABIT

"We are the sum of our actions, therefore our habits make all the difference."

-- *Aristotle*

"I never remember feeling tired by work, though idleness exhausts me completely."

-- *Sir Arthur Conan Doyle*

Is it a bad hand? A bad deal?

Or is it an opportunity to play the hand that's dealt you? Everyone says "Life ain't fair" -- what's your point? The good guy didn't win. Why? It wasn't the good guy's turn to win? Look at your own life. That's the only one that matters. Life ain't fair for others -- get out of your rut.

I had two choices as I looked at the cards I was dealt. I could wallow in my self-pity and say, "Oh, poor pitiful me. I am a poverty-stricken, ghetto-living, fatherless child." Or I could look at my circumstances and use them as motivation to succeed in life. Hopefully by this point you've concluded, if you didn't earlier, which choice I made without me telling you.

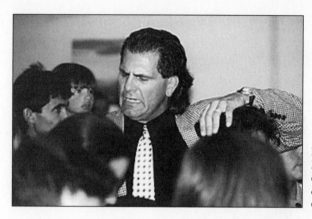

Nikita, sporting the Mel Gibson look, encourages the crowd in Bogotá, Colombia (1997).

What about you? Have you made the right choices? Because it's really not about the cards you're dealt, it really is about how you play those cards. Once you look at your situation, think about it and analyze it. The next logical step would be to take action. Do you? Or are you caught up in the "roll over" factor? Roll over enough days and it becomes a habit. People think, and people are told, it takes approximately twenty-eight days to form a habit.

Do you wake up in the morning and not want to? How many years have you been doing that? What separates the winners from the losers are those who make the decision to get out of bed. I got out of bed this morning and completed another chapter of this book. I wanted to sleep in, but my desire to complete this book to benefit people like you, the reader, was greater than my desire to sleep.

I've been working out and lifting weights for over thirty years. You might say it's become a habit. How did it become a habit? It became a habit because I decided that I didn't want to be a 98-pound weakling.

What have you been procrastinating about? Why are you still waiting for the train to roll into the station? Why are you still waiting for the ship to come into the harbor? Stop procrastinating. Make the decision that you're going to be successful as a businessperson, a wife, a husband, a parent, a mentor, or as a friend. Once you make that decision, as Winston Churchill once said, "Never give up." By your persistence, your choice will become a habit.

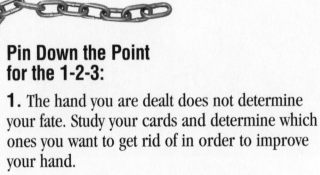

Pin Down the Point
for the 1-2-3:

1. The hand you are dealt does not determine your fate. Study your cards and determine which ones you want to get rid of in order to improve your hand.

2. Success habits take slightly more than twenty-eight days to develop. They take a lifetime.

3. "Never give up." -- Winston Churchill

••• *Finally the bell tolled, and it was time for Nikita and Ivan to enter the ring. As they were escorted in to the music of the Soviet national anthem, a sea of boos followed them. As Nikita stood stoically in the ring with that stone-cold look that only he could portray, the boos continued for several minutes. Ivan stirred an even greater reaction from the fans as he gestured and shouted at those in the front rows* •••

Chapter 36

FROM SUCCESS TO CHAMPION

"The obvious goals were there -- state champion, NCAA champion, Olympic champion. To get there I had to set an everyday goal, which was to push myself to exhaustion or, in other words, to work so hard in practice that someone would have to carry me off the mat."

-- Dan Gable, former wrestler

"Teamwork is the fuel that allows common people to attain uncommon results."

-- Nikita Koloff

You don't just put the belt on, you earn the belt. You work for the belt. You struggle for the belt. You dream about the belt. But there are steps that you have to take to get the belt. Take a look at mine and figure out what yours need to be.

Physical self-discipline was first. It all started at the age of twelve when I picked up that first body-building magazine. There was immediate intrigue, attraction, and desire as I looked at the magazine. This took me to the point where I went and spent my own money on a 110-pound weight set. I continued to read about how to lift, what to do, and what not to do to develop muscles.

I enjoyed working out. I enjoyed the physical "pump" that I got from it and the feeling of accomplishment at the end of a workout. Not long after, even at an early age, I began to see some difference in my physical stature. The *Ironman* magazine was the catalyst behind it all.

The mental followed along with the physical. As I saw improvements in my body, it was enough encouragement to keep me going. The physical improvements helped develop my mental attitude and motivated me to work out.

My oldest brother had been an athlete in high school. He always said to me, "Athletes don't drink. Athletes don't smoke." And it stuck with me all my life. As I progressed through middle school and high school, of course I gravitated to other jocks and athletes to hang out with, as opposed to "the other crowd."

As time progressed, I began to develop the necessary physical and mental attitude, and the self-discipline. I became a regular subscriber to *Ironman* and other body-building magazines. I began to talk with others who were weightlifting to brainstorm ideas to keep improving. I was always motivated to look for the cutting edge that could bring me to the next level of improvement.

Diet fell into place naturally after reading and educating myself with the magazines. Gerry McFarland was there to help me lower my body fat and work on my diet. He was always there for me to ask questions when I needed guidance. Magazines and mentors became a critical part in developing the fully rounded person. Mentors, magazines, and the obvious physical results that I was experiencing kept me going. The increase in the amount of weights I could lift and the increase in the bulge of my biceps also encouraged and motivated me.

Training partners are essential if you're going to move from success to champion. I gained knowledge from books and magazines, but I got my motivation from my partners, who were major catalysts in my success. They constantly challenged me and pushed me when I was tired and didn't want to be there. I always picked a partner who would push me without getting me mad at him. And they always pushed me further than I could have gone on my own.

They provided discipline -- my partners would hold me accountable for showing up, and from the diet standpoint -- they made sure I would stick to what we had agreed to do.

From a mental standpoint, my training partners gave me positive reinforcement, and I succeeded more times than I failed in making the lift. Many times, I exceeded even a partner's expectations. When I said I wanted to get four reps, and he said, no, you are going to get five, I would end up getting six. You can be successful on your own, but a partner who motivates you, pushes you, challenges you, and holds you accountable will enable you to move from being successful to becoming a true champion no matter what your endeavor.

Pin Down the Point
for the 1-2-3:

1. Physical, mental, and spiritual improvement are a blend. The success blend.

2. Have a "training" partner. Someone who will encourage you, someone who will stay on you, and someone you can share the struggle with.

3. To be a champion you need to get past the rule: Life ain't fair.

● ● ● *As the music shifted from the Soviet national anthem to the "Star-Spangled Banner" (appropriate music for this July 4th celebration), the voices echoed in the night air and shifted from a sea of boos to ear-deafening cheers. Soon a helicopter appeared on the horizon, making its way to the infield of the stadium* ● ● ●

Chapter 37

SUCCESS IS NOT COMPLICATED.

"Winning is not the only thing that counts. There are times when the loser profits more in experience than the winner."

-- *William Muldoon, former wrestler*

Gitomer: Everyone is struggling for success. Everyone is wrestling with success. Everyone is doing their best to be as successful as they can possibly be. Some love their success when they arrive, some hate it. The reason they hate it is that they didn't love it when they started out.

What you will read about in this chapter is a game plan full of the obvious. But the obvious has more truth to it than any other series of words. *Think and Grow Rich, How to Win Friends and Influence People*, and *The Power of Positive Thinking* are full of the obvious. If you read those books cover to cover, there is not a single "Aha!" There are, however, a thousand lessons about what you already know but are not doing.

If you are really looking for success and want to struggle less, wrestle less, then take another dose of the obvious. Below are 14.5 obvious things to do. If you do them, they will help you pass the others who only know them.

1. The idea. Everyone is in search of an idea and most people already have the idea but have not yet put it into place. The business they are going to start, they book they are going to read or write, the client they are going to get, the sale they are going to make, the weights they are going to lift ... you know. You've got tons of them. You may refer to it as a goal. You may refer to it as a wish. But in essence, it's your idea of how you want to achieve. What most people do not do is write it down in detail. And even fewer people break it down into small chunks. They have a big idea without a small game plan to achieve it. You know the old joke: *How do you eat an elephant? One bite at a time.* The reason it's old is because it's true. You don't write a book, you write a paragraph. You don't get a client, you make a phone call. You don't lose fifty pounds, you lose two ounces.

2. The attitude. Everybody has an attitude. The only question is, positive or negative? Most people are negative. That's why most people fail. Get an attitude book collection beginning with *The Little Engine That Could.* Read that twice a day till you finally "think you can." Most people read the book and get nothing out of it. Every time a child is born to a friend of mine, the child gets a set of bookends and one book, *The Little Engine That Could.* I inscribe in the book, "This is not just a book for a kid, it's a philosophy for a lifetime." And that's the closest thing to truth I've ever written. I have always lived by the mantra, "I think I can." Oh, I don't succeed every time, but that does not stop me from thinking that I can the next time. When all else had failed me in my life, attitude continued to lead me to success. And so it will for you.

3. Do you love it? How many people do you know who hate their job? Answer: lots! How many people do you know who hate their job and are the world's best at it? Answer: None. Jeez, I wonder if that's a coincidence. The people who love what they do are 1,000 times more likely to succeed at what they do than someone who begrudgingly goes to work. If you really want to succeed, pick something that you love to do and success will be yours from the first day, with or without money.

4. The dream MUST be bigger than the dreamer. Small

dreams, small success. Big dreams, big success. Even if you don't go for your big dream all at once, have one that you can hang your hat on. Have one that you can clearly see. Have one that you can clearly visualize. And have one that you will eventually live. If you can begin by achieving your small dreams, I promise you, you will be able to achieve your big ones.

5. Focus around learning -- not knowing (Be the student of success). I know too many people who already know everything.

Many of them sit in my seminar audiences. What they don't understand is the difference between knowing and doing. I don't care if you know it. What I care is, how good you are at it, and are you doing your best at it? The best thing I ever did for my own success was to believe at twenty years old that I knew everything, and to realize at twenty-one years old that I knew nothing. From the age of twenty-one, I've had one quest and one major goal: Learn something new every day. That has led me down the path of success, regardless of whether I succeeded or failed. Every episode was a lesson. And so I challenge you to learn something new every day, regardless of the fact that you already know everything.

6. The method method. When Scott Simpson became Nikita

Koloff, he didn't just change his name. He changed his character. He changed his persona. He changed his method of communication. He transformed himself into the character of Nikita Koloff. By immersing himself, by living the part, he became more successful than any other wrestler of his time. Even though he hasn't wrestled in more than a decade, people still stop him on the street, in a restaurant, or in a hotel lobby. He was hateable and he was lovable because he lived the part. In acting it's referred to as "method acting." The most famous actors of our time, Marlon Brando, Robert DeNiro, Dustin Hoffman, all subscribe to that philosophy -- live the part. For me, method acting occurred when I was trying to achieve positive attitude. I started out with a lousy one, and when I began listening to tapes and reading books, I realized I was not going to change in a day. So I began "method acting." Or, using a less

sophisticated term, I faked it. I was happy to everyone and
everything. I looked at the good in things even though, coming from
New Jersey for my first twenty-four years, I predominantly saw the
bad. But after six months or so of faking it, my attitude actually
changed from negative to positive where it has remained for the last
30-plus years and will stay with me for the rest of time. All because
I chose to live the part of positive at a time when I was negative.
Oh, by the way, did my friends think I was nuts? Every single one of
them. There's one difference between them and me now -- I'm still
happy. My warning to you is that the method method is not easy.
But the good news is that it works. It worked for Nikita Koloff, it
worked for me, and it can work for you if you dedicate yourself to it.

7. The personal passion (weekend work). What do you do on
the weekend? If you are looking for areas of passion, you only have
to look at the things that you love to do. Might be hunting, might
be golfing, might be traveling, might be reading. But whatever it is,
you're passionate for it. Imagine what could happen if you took
that same passion and converted it to your career. How much more
successful would that make you? The secret of success is passion-
conversion. Ask yourself why you love what you do with passion.
Look at the ends that you are willing to go to to play golf in the
rain, and then you'll know what it takes to be successful at your
career. A game plan with no passion will never be fulfilled.

8. The struggle. Most people have no appreciation for the fun
they can have while they're broke. Part of the reason is that their
attitude stinks to begin with and they think that if they just had
some money, they would have a better outlook. That's a bunch of
crap. I'm sure you've heard the expression, "Smell the roses along
the way." That's what the struggle is all about. Enjoying it. Taking
time to step back and realize that the struggle is the best part of
the process. That the struggle is the part where you learn the most.
Sure, it's work. Sure, there are lean times. Hey, Sparky, that's why
they call it the struggle. All successful people look back on their
struggle with the fondest of memories. My challenge to you is:
Don't just make it a memory. Make it an enjoyable experience.

9. The feeling of success. Have you ever had a gut feeling that something was going to go right or something was going to go wrong? And your feelings turned out to be true? No one knows why but the process is instinctive. You "feel it." Success is almost the same thing. The way you can feel success is to constantly keep in mind past successes. Each day, draw upon how you did it. Why it was good. How you felt. And how to repeat that process. Success is a feeling, and you already know what it is. The challenge is to keep it in the front of your mind even in the toughest of times.

10. The belief. I believe in myself as much as anything in my belief system. And so must you. I believe my company is the best in the world, and so must you. I believe my products and services are the best in the world, and so must you. In order to achieve any level of success, your belief system must be with you every step of the way. People will sense your belief, or lack thereof, and will act accordingly. If you're only in it to "make some money," people will sense that, too. Very few people understand how important a belief system is as they wrestle with their success process, as they wrestle with their success dreams. Your challenge is to develop the belief system before you start the success process. The deeper the belief, the higher the achievement.

11. The common sense. In the heat of battle is when you must remain the calmest. And when you're wrestling or struggling for success, it may be your biggest single challenge. Not yelling, not ranting, not losing your cool. The more negative energy you exude, the more difficult it is for you to be rational about what's going on, and worse, what the ramifications are of what will occur next. If you don't know how to meditate, spend at least fifteen minutes a day in tranquility so that you can recall the feeling when everything around you is on fire. The least-used of all the senses is common sense. Yet it remains your elusive butterfly as you wrestle for success.

12. The pride. Remember when your kid took his first step? Or got an A? Or hit a home run? Remember how you felt? You probably couldn't wait to tell everybody and their dog. You probably took a bunch of photos or even movies. You probably still show the movie. That's pride. Genuine pride. And if you're going to achieve success, you're going to have to develop that sense of pride in every one of your achievements, no matter how large or how small. And you don't have to brag to other people, hey, I did this, hey, I did that. Some might misconstrue that as arrogance. Pride is something that you carry with you. Pride is something that you feel. And the more you capture it and keep it to yourself, the more others will feel it in you without you ever having to say a word about it. Your challenge is to stand up straight, stick out your chest, and close your mouth.

13. The fulfillment (beyond success). I'm going to issue you two more challenges. The first one is about "beyond success." Also known as fulfillment. Fulfillment is a feeling of happiness and of completeness combined with pride that comes with success. Success alone has nothing to do with fulfillment. You may have a lot of money and be the most unhappy person on the planet, and that's because you failed to achieve mastery in the twelve elements listed prior to this one. If you're not happy with your money, then you will not understand the difference between success and fulfillment. If your bank account is tall and your temper is short, your fulfillment is low. If your balance sheet is good and your relationship with your kids is bad, then you will not have achieved fulfillment. You may be successful, but you are not fulfilled. Fulfillment is difficult to describe. But you'll know it when you feel it. And it is my greatest hope that each of you gets to feel it in your own way. Fulfillment has nothing to do with money and only something to do with success. Fulfillment has everything to do with how you feel about yourself when you are alone in the bathroom looking in the mirror at the beginning and at the end of each day.

14. Service to others leads to fulfillment. There is a 5,000-year-old ancient Chinese proverb that says, "To serve is to rule." It does not mean that you will rule the world. It does mean that you will rule yourself. Your self-discipline. Your pride of accomplishment. And your willingness to help others. If it has ever made you feel good to help someone when they're down, to give someone information they can use when they need it, to be behind the scenes and watch someone else succeed, and feel good about it, then you will know the meaning of, "To serve is to rule." Your challenge is to live the proverb.

14.5 Hard work makes luck. Everyone is looking to "get lucky." For many people, it manifests in the number of lottery tickets they buy each week, hoping to "get lucky." Me, I've already hit the lottery. No, not that lottery, that's just money. I'm talking about the lottery that gives me everything that I want. That's a lottery anyone can win. Somebody once asked the old comedian Jackie Mason, "How do you become an overnight success?" "Easy," he said, "just work your butt off for twenty years and presto! You're an overnight success." That's pretty much my story. But I was helped along the way by an old mentor in Chicago named Mel Green. I was standing outside a hotel doorway at 5:30 A.M. one February morning, waiting for Mel to pick me up. It was snowing sideways and dark like the middle of the night. He drove up right on time. I jumped in the car. And as we talked, I thought back on several projects of his that had all turned to gold. "Man, you're lucky," I said. Without flinching, he spun around and looked at me and said, "Hard work makes luck." Ever since that day, I've doubled my work effort. And while I admit to you that everything has not been a success, in the same breath I will tell you that I have had nothing but luck.

Pin Down the Point for the 1-2-3:

1. Re-read this chapter ten times. Then re-read it once a month for a year. See how much closer you are to your own success each time you re-read one of the elements. See how much self-improvement you have made each time you read one of the elements. If re-reading is a "pain," it means you're not very far along on the success path.

2. You already know how to succeed. Now all you have to do is take success actions.

3. Life ain't fair.

●●● As the helicopter landed, the red carpet was rolled out, the door opened, and Ric Flair, the Nature Boy, made his entrance into the ring, sporting the diamond studded, blue and silver robe that only he could wear. As he made his way down the red carpet with music blasting, an entourage of police escorts held back the fans. He entered the ring ●●●

Chapter  **38**

THE FORMULA FOR SUCCESS

"When you finally decide how successful
you really want to be, you've got to set
priorities. Then each and every day,
you've got to take care of the top ones.
The lower ones may fall behind, but you
can't let the top ones slip. You don't
forget about the lower ones though
because they can add up to hurt you.
Just take care of the top ones first."

-- Dan Gable, former wrestler

The "You're Crazy" Rule: You say you're gonna do
something, someone else says, "You're crazy."

No dad
(You'll never make it out of the ghetto.)

No future
(You'll never come back/recover after the injury.)

No ability
(You'll never wrestle. You already have a good job.)

My rule of thumb has always been, when someone says "You're crazy," it has always meant that I'm on the right path.

Les Brown said to me, "Never let someone else's opinion of you become your reality."

I had a choice. Three times they told me I was crazy. No dad, no future, no ability. I was just a youngster the first time I heard it (someone else's opinion). I chose not to believe it. I was that eighteen-year-old punk kid the second time. I chose not to believe it. I was a twenty-four-year-old on my way to maturity (or so I thought) the third time I heard it. I chose not to believe it.

My formula for success: Develop a "no quit" policy. I could have quit dreaming about leaving the ghetto and just resolved that this was it, but I didn't. I could have quit lifting the weights, but I didn't. I could have quit playing football and pursued something else, but I didn't. I could have believed them when they said I was crazy to wrestle, but I didn't.

We've given you a lot of meat to chew on in the previous chapters. It's our hope that you'll take what fits you and create your own formula for success. This book doesn't have the six keys to success or the seven keys to victory. It contains the thoughts and experiences of two men who've had success and would like to share that information with you. Get started on your own formula now. What are you waiting for?

Maybe you're waiting for Gitomer's formula. Here it is:

I wanna be a success!
I wanna be a success!

So, what's the secret of sales success? Well -- it's not a single secret -- it's a secret formula.

Here are the 18.5 Secrets of Success: (And more important, are you a master of each of these characteristics?)

1. Believe you can. You have the mental posture for success -- believing you are capable of achieving it. This belief must extend to your product and company. A strong belief system seems obvious -- but few people possess it. Too many salespeople look outside (for the money they can make) rather than look inside (for the money they can earn). Believing that you're the best and that you're capable of achievement is the hardest thing to do. It requires daily dedication to self-support, self-encouragement, and positive self-talk.

2. Create the environment. The right home and work environment will encourage you. Supportive spouse, family members, and co-workers will make the road to success a smooth ride. It's up to you to create it.

3. Have the right associations. Hang around the right people -- other successful people. Network where their best customers and prospects go. Join the right associations. Make the right friends. Stay away from poison people -- the ones who can't seem to get anywhere. Have a mentor or three. Who do you hang around with? They are who you are likely to become.

4. Expose yourself to what's new. If you're not learning every day -- your competition is. New information is essential to success. (Unless you're like most salespeople who already know everything -- lucky you.)

5. Plan for the day. Since you don't know on which day success will occur, you'd better be ready every day. Prepare with education. Plan with goals and the details for their achievement. Learning and goals are the surest methods to be ready for your success.

6. Become valuable. The more valuable you become, the more the marketplace will reward you. Give first. Become known as a resource, not a salesperson. Your value is linked to your knowledge and your willingness to help others.

7. Have the answers your prospects and customers need.
The more you can solve problems, the easier the path you will
have to sales success. Prospects don't want facts, they want answers.
In order to have those answers, you must have superior knowledge
about what you do -- and explain it in terms of how the prospect
uses what you do.

8. Recognize opportunity. Stay alert for the situations that can
create success opportunities. The little-known key is to get and
maintain a positive attitude. Attitude allows you to see the
possibilities when opportunity strikes -- because it often shows
up in the form of adversity.

9. Take advantage of opportunity. First, recognize it (because
again, it often shows up disguised in the form of adversity.) Second,
act on it. Opportunity is elusive. It exists all over the place, but very
few can see it. Some people fear it because it involves change; most
don't believe they are capable of achievement.

10. Take responsibility. We all blame others to a degree.
Blame is tied to success in reverse proportion. The lower your
degree of blame -- the higher the degree of success you'll achieve.
Get the job done yourself no matter what. Petty blame is rampant
and the biggest waste of time. Don't blame others or yourself. Take
responsibility for your actions and decisions. Blaming others is an
easy thing to do but leads to a path of mediocrity. Successful people
take responsibility for everything they do **AND** everything that
happens to them.

11. Take action. *Just do it* (Nike) was the expression for the
90s. Actions are the only way to bridge plans and goals with
accomplishment. Nothing happens until you do something to make
it happen -- every day.

12. Make mistakes. The best teacher is failure. It's the rudest of
awakenings and the breeding ground for self-determination. Don't
think of them as mistakes -- think of them as learning experiences
not to be repeated.

13. Be willing to risk. This is the most crucial factor. *No risk, no reward* is the biggest understatement in the business world. It should be stated -- *No risk, no nothing.* Taking chances is a common thread among every successful person. *No risk, no reward* the saying goes -- and it's true. Most people won't risk because they think they *fear the unknown.* The real reason people won't risk is that they lack the preparation and education that breeds the self-confidence (self-belief) to take a chance. Risk is the basis of success. If you want to succeed, you'd better be willing to risk whatever it takes to get there.

14. Keep your eye on the prize. Post your goals. Stay focused on your dreams and they will become reality. Too many foolish diversions will take you off the path.

15. Balance yourself. Your physical, spiritual, and emotional health are vital to your success quest. Plan your time to allow your personal goals to be synergized with your work goals.

16. Invest, don't spend. There should be a 10 to 20 percent gap between earning and spending. Clip your credit cards in half and make a few investments -- with professional guidance.

17. Stick with it until you win. Most people fail because they quit too soon. Don't let that be you. Make a plan **AND** a commitment to see the plan through -- no matter what. Don't quit on the ten-yard line. Have whatever it takes to score.

18. Develop and maintain a positive attitude. Surprisingly, this is not a common characteristic. By the time many make it to the top, they have developed irreversible cynicism. But positive attitude makes achieving success much easier -- and more fun.

18.5 Ignore idiots and zealots. These people will try to rain on your parade (discourage you) because they have no parade of their own. Avoid them at all costs.

See, I told you -- no revelations. Okay, so if these secrets to success seem so simple, how come they're so difficult to master? Answer -- your lack of personal self-discipline and a dedication to life-long learning. Oh yeah, that.

I am consistently amazed and disappointed at the small number of people willing to execute the simple daily self-disciplines needed to reach higher levels of success. They know it will bring them the success they dream about, yet they fail to execute.

In sales, or any business effort, or career position, the person who will emerge victorious most of the time is the person who wants it the most. Victory does not always go to the swift (hare vs. tortoise), victory does not always go to the powerful (David vs. Goliath), and victory does not always go to the lowest price (Yugo vs. Mercedes).

The victory we call success goes to the best-prepared, self-believing, right-associated, self-taught, responsible person who sees the opportunity and is willing to take a risk to seize it -- sometimes a big risk. Is that you?

That's the secret -- and it's not real complicated. It's not nuclear physics or brain surgery. And now that I've shared it with thousands of people, you'd think there would be a surge in the ratio of successful salespeople. Nope.

The reason the success formula is considered a secret is that it remains an enigma. It seems that there are very few people who are willing to put forth the *effort* to get from where they are to where they want to be. Most make excuses and blame others for their own poor choices.

The biggest secret
(and the biggest obstacle)
to success is *you.*
The formula is there
for everyone to know --
BUT, there's a
big difference between
knowing what to do
and doing it.

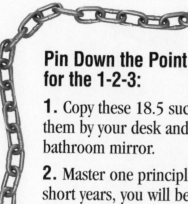

Pin Down the Point for the 1-2-3:

1. Copy these 18.5 success principles and put them by your desk and post them on your bathroom mirror.

2. Master one principle every thirty days. In two short years, you will be ready to begin your success quest as a master rather than a novice.

3. The secret of success is: There's no secret of success.

••• *Nikita remained standing in the center of the ring with his cold, stoic look, watching the frenzy that the Nature Boy created. Uncle Ivan did his best to make sure that special referee David Crockett would call a fair match. Crocket escorted Uncle Ivan to his place at ringside and demanded that he not move from his chair. He instructed Nikita to remove his infamous chain from around his neck. Nikita placed it over the ring post as was his custom to do. Upon completing his inspection of each wrestler's boots and tights (making sure neither had any foreign objects) and amidst a deafening sea of cheers for Nature Boy Ric Flair, Crockett called for the opening bell. And the match began* •••

Part

6

Epilogue of Thoughts and Insights

NOW THAT YOU'VE READ THE LESSONS, YOU NEED TO GLUE THEM TOGETHER WITH INSIGHT.

Your thought processes and your ability to execute are in direct proportion to your success. Every time you come to business crossroads, you have to choose a direction. You have to choose a path.

Remember the Cheshire cat? You know, the one from *Alice's Adventures in Wonderland*. His famous quote is, "When you don't know where you're going, any road will do."

Insight will carry you to the next level of success. The key to insight is thinking. Take a moment right now and look in your day planner. See how many times you have the word "think" in there. For most people it's none.

Imagine that. Thinking is critical to your success yet you've set aside no time to do it. Seems pretty stupid, doesn't it? Well, don't worry, now is your chance. As you complete the last pages of this book, your first action step is to set aside think-time each day even if it's only fifteen or twenty minutes.

The last key is to turn your thoughts and insights into reality. And the answer to that timeless challenge can be found at the end of this sentence and throughout the book: *Work hard.*

Chapter  39

SUCCESS LESSONS FROM "GETTING OVER"

"I have never in my life envied a human
being who led an easy life; I have envied
a great many people who lead difficult
lives and lead them well."

-- Theodore Roosevelt, former wrestler

What is getting over? If you've ever watched professional wrestling,
and you "hate" one of the characters, that means the wrestler
"got over." It means you bought his character. He may be the nicest,
gentlest guy in the world after he leaves the stadium. But his
character was so compelling that you believed it. You bought it.
He got over.

Getting over is an important element of success. It doesn't mean
you have to fake who you are. It does mean you have to be
passionate about who you are so that others believe in you as much
as you believe in yourself.

Here's how it works in wrestling: It started with an idea, a story line.
Don said to Sergeant Slaughter, "I'll go team up with Ivan and
become an American turncoat. We'll win the tag-team titles. Then
what if we find a nephew for Ivan and he becomes our partner?"
Slaughter said, "It sounds like a good start."

It continued with an angle. "Eventually the Russians turn against me," said Don Kernodle. He called in the cavalry, Sergeant Slaughter. The angle created instant interest from the fans. You couldn't ask for a more classic angle, the Soviets against the Americans.

Now it was time to "get it over" and sell it to the crowd. We promoted the angle through television via interviews, and that drew the people to the arenas. The people bought into the whole angle. It did sell-out business.

What do you learn from this? You've got to get yourself "over." When you date, you have a story. Your story. Then, using creativity, you think of an angle to "sell yourself" to the other person. When he or she buys into the story, you build your relationship from there.

The key to success is to "get over." If you're a parent, you want to get over with your children. If you're a child, it's with your parents. Or perhaps, it's with your spouse or as an employee with your boss or vice versa. Hopefully, you get the picture.

How does this relate to business? I owned several gyms (the story line). I promoted health to everyone (the angle). I creatively advertised using billboards, newspapers, and radio. I sold my product (memberships) because I showed people why they needed to work out and the benefits from working out. If you build it, they will come. And they did.

So what are you doing to get yourself "over"? What's your story? What's your angle? How creative are you? And the ultimate question is: Are they buying?

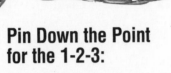

Pin Down the Point
for the 1-2-3:

1. Self-belief leads to passion, passion leads to getting over.

2. Your presentation skills play a major role in your success. Presentation skills are the least-studied of all the success skills. By joining Toastmasters (www.toastmasters.org), you can propel yourself to the front of the room.

3. If your "story angle" is not working, if people aren't buying what you're saying, don't blame them, it ain't their fault … it's yours.

Bonus Point: Sell yourself in a way that the other person buys.

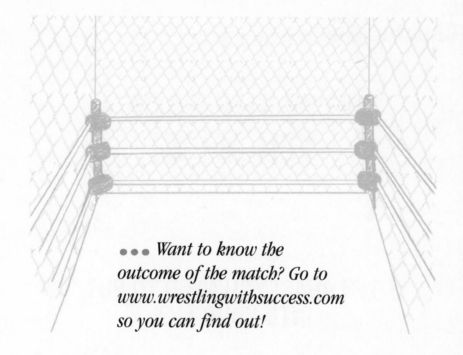

••• *Want to know the outcome of the match? Go to www.wrestlingwithsuccess.com so you can find out!*

Chapter 40

PIE IN THE FACE --
TEN AHAS!

"The older I get, the tougher I was ..."
-- Old wrestling adage

TEN AHAS! YOU NEED TO PUT
INTO YOUR LIFE

You may have missed these -- but we believe you need to act on these now ... or risk losing the match to a "no name."

1. Oftentimes in life, there is someone in the middle, a referee of sorts, who by his or her actions can give you defeat or victory. Make certain that you build relationships with all people in your path.

2. Never let someone else's opinion become your reality.

3. Be ready for opportunity when it strikes -- get ready now.

4. It's not only how much money you make, it's how you look in your wrestling tights. How do you look?

5. Professional wrestling is not fixed. The outcomes are predetermined. Even though Nikita knew how every match was going to come out, he was prepared. How good are you at predetermining your outcomes?

6. Whether the crowd is cheering for you or cheering against you, you have to be a winner in your own mind.

7. When things go wrong and you are in pain, physical pain, the most important things in your life will flash in front of you. The problem you may have is not being in pain enough and not focusing on what is really important.

8. When you're in serious pain, you can see the future. Your career. Your children. Your lost opportunities. And you see very clearly what you wish you had done. Stop wishing, start doing.

9. When things go wrong in business, most people get angry. Anger blocks clear thinking. Convert the anger into determination in order to make your best judgments at moments of truth.

10. Most people leave their shoulders on the mat when they hear the count of two.

Pin Down the Point for the 1-2-3:

1. Whether the crowd is cheering or booing, you can always win if you just cheer for yourself.

2. Rise up before the count of three, even if you are already at the count of two. As long as the referee is still counting, you still have a chance to win.

3. Anger blocks clear thinking. Anger blocks creative thinking. I'm not saying never get angry. All I'm saying is that these are the consequences of anger.

Chapter 41

MOVING FROM SUCCESS TO SIGNIFICANCE AND FULFILLMENT

"God gave man work, not to burden him, but to bless him. Useful work, willingly, cheerfully, effectively done, has always been the finest expression of the human spirit."

-- Walter R. Courtenay

"Serendipity is God's way of remaining anonymous."

-- Jeffrey Gitomer

Koloff: In my short stay on planet Earth, I've led a very interesting and exciting life. I've gone from the ghetto, to the suburb, or affectionately, from the outhouse to the penthouse.

I've excelled in the weight room, had outstanding years on the football field, and won many championships and accolades. I achieved in the classroom, becoming an academic All-American (my picture still hangs in the college field house) and graduating with honors as a Cum Laude.

I had an illustrious wrestling career, winning many championship belts including world championship titles five times. I wrestled in forty-three of the fifty states, and I traveled to numerous other nations for business, pleasure, and ministry, experiencing many different cultures as well as different cuisines.

I was a finalist for the *Rocky IV* movie as the Russian character Ivan Drago. I've owned health clubs and invested in many other business ventures. I have married the most unique, gorgeous woman in the world and have four beautiful daughters. I have indeed lived an exciting life. You might say I've had a very successful life considering my humble beginnings. Yet, amidst all the success, I found myself in search of something bigger.

In October of 1993, after retiring from wrestling, I stepped into another squared circle for the wrestling match of a lifetime. This was not your typical wrestling ring. This squared circle was a church.

Ric Flair is famous for saying, "If you want to be the man, you have to beat the man and walk that aisle." I didn't walk an aisle on that October morning to meet Ric Flair, The Rock, Stone Cold Steve Austin, Hulk Hogan, Sting, or any other wrestler in the ring. I went forward to bow a knee to the champion for the world, Jesus Christ. It was on that day that I went from being successful to becoming fulfilled.

Yes, I tasted success early in this journey called life and learned a few things along the way. An African proverb says, "Each step leads to another." And how true it is.

From an early age, I began to visualize my success and set goals, and I've been fortunate to see many of them come to fruition. It's been said, to accomplish goals you must begin with the end in mind. This is a task you must develop if you have yet to learn it. You must visualize yourself climbing the ladder of success one step at a time, one day at a time, every day of your life.

Perhaps you've heard it said, success is not a destination, it's a personal journey. Identifying a starting point of a journey is just as important as determining the destination. Each of us is born to shape a personal destiny. The depth and extent of that destiny are measured by our level of fulfillment.

I recently returned from a mission trip to South Africa. While there, I sat at dinner one night with a friend, Ron Davis, a banker from North Carolina. Ron is success personified. He is co-chairman and president of a bank and holds a strong position on five boards of directors for various successful companies.

I heard recently that Ron has resigned all his positions. When I queried him, he said, "I've been working in banking for thirty-three years. I work from 6 A.M. to 11 P.M. attending one meeting after another. I have missed my children growing up and missed spending quality time with my wife."

I thought to myself as he spoke about the sacrifices we make for success. He continued by saying it was time to make a change. He was ready to move from success to significance. He was ready to make a real difference in people's lives.

He has indeed resigned from all his business obligations. He has taken a new position as fiduciary director of a nonprofit organization called Umbono, a project that produces micro-businesses for the people of South Africa. It is a project that is creating jobs to uplift and empower the people while bringing education and filling many needs.

After thirty-three years in the business world, Ron has received a revelation that many who attain his level of success have realized. Success can leave you empty and unfulfilled. Only when you do something of real significance will you truly reach fulfillment. Ron is quickly becoming a world changer and a history maker. His wife and his daughter were able to travel with him to South Africa. I can identify with Ron's story because I too have moved from success to significance and fulfillment.

You are the sum total of all your choices. You achieve what you believe in, look for, and work for. Let me ask you some serious questions, "Do you want to be a world changer?" "Do you want to be a world champion in life?" Champions are not those who never fail, they are those who never quit.

Every man and woman is limited by three things; the knowledge in his or her mind, the strength of his or her character, and the principles upon which he or she is building his or her life. The best measure of success and fulfillment is what you're doing compared to your true potential. If you continue to do what you've always done, you'll continue to get what you've always gotten. The more you do the right things, the more you'll get the right results.

Gitomer: Too many people become successful and are angry about it. You have seen many wealthy people acting like jerks, mad at everything and everyone, and clearly not having a good time at life. You know the old expression: crying with a silver spoon in your mouth.

Fulfillment is happiness beyond success. Fulfillment is the feeling that you get when you are successful and proud of it. Writing a book can make you successful. Seeing your book in your bookstore as soon as you walk in is fulfillment. Having someone come up to you with your book under his or her arm and asking for an autograph is fulfillment.

Your attitude of acceptance when these chances for fulfillment occur is your choice. Ever see an athlete refuse to autograph a piece of paper for a kid? That's an unfulfilled athlete.

I never understood fulfillment until one day my dad called me and said, "Son, I'm proud of you."

As you seek success, it is important that you understand *why* you want to be successful. Not for the money, but rather, what you will do with the money. Who you will help with the money. That's fulfillment.

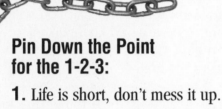

Pin Down the Point
for the 1-2-3:

1. Life is short, don't mess it up.

2. Champions are not those who never fail, they are those who never quit.

3. Take a piece of paper and list five things that will fulfill you, then go backwards and figure out what you have to do to make those five things a reality. Do them.

Nikita spreads his message across the United States and overseas.

Chapter  42

CAREERS ARE SHORT -- LIFE IS SHORTER.

"When the One Great Scorer comes to mark against your name, He writes -- not that you won or lost -- but how you played the game."

-- Grantland Rice

I had someone close to me die at the age of twenty-six. The cancer was detected at the age of twenty-four. After two long years of battles, it was over. It was my first inside glimpse of how short life can really be. In the last ten years, there have been more than twenty-five wrestlers who have died before the age of forty-five. It is said that life is like a vapor, a blink, a twinkling of the eye, or a blowing of the wind.

My priorities have drastically changed over the last few years. There was a time earlier in life when I thought my career was the absolute most important thing in my life. As I've matured, I've come to realize that relationships take precedence over everything else.

Today, I watched my youngest daughter's first basketball game. Soon, I'll watch another daughter's first music recital. It seems like yesterday when I witnessed my oldest daughter's and second daughter's first cheerleading games. I could have been many other places, but none as memorable as those when I watched my children grow.

I am reminded of the Harry Chapin song, "Cat's in the Cradle." "When you coming home, Dad? I don't know when. But we'll get together then. You know we'll have a good time then." Well, Dad never came home. For me or for the boy in the song. He grew up to be just like Dad. I was determined not to. I was determined to be there to see my children grow. I am determined to take my wife out on dates.

Why have I taken the time to build an inner circle of friends like Don K., Don E., Tim, Todd, Terence, and Jeffrey? It's said, "There is wisdom in the multitude of counsel." I am without a doubt a blessed and fortunate man to have many quality people around me. But they didn't just show up. I worked for it.

Just a few years ago, I made the decision that I wanted to make a difference in this life I've been given. At first I wanted to leave a legacy, but now I want to live a legacy that I can in turn leave a greater legacy. What about you? Why do you do what you do? Aren't you tired of treading water? Why flow with the current like everyone else? Swim upstream. There's a championship belt up there (be careful of the bears standing in the water waiting to eat you).

Your championship match is part of your life's journey. To get to the championship match, you'd better be ready to wrestle. Then, and only then, can you win the match, win the belt, strap the belt on, and keep the belt on. Be sure to let others share in the victory, and follow your destiny. I made the transition from weight-lifter guy, to weight-lifter-off-the-other-guy's-shoulder guy. It's time for you to make the same transition.

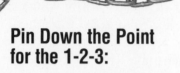

Pin Down the Point
for the 1-2-3:

1. Ask yourself, "Do I have my priorities in order?"

2. Life offers very few "onlys." Never miss an only. An only can be a kid's dance recital, trick-or-treating, family reunions, high school reunions, a championship ballgame for your home team, and other significant events that only come along once. How many onlys have you missed? Stop missing them.

3. Don't leave a legacy, live a legacy. Then you'll have a legacy to leave.

Koloff with his true success, his wife Victoria.

Chapter  43

SHORTCUTS

There are no shortcuts.

ACKNOWLEDGMENTS: KOLOFF

My family: **Victoria**, **Teryn**, **Tawni**, **Kendra**, and **Kolby**. Thanks for your sacrifices while I worked on this project. You all were my greatest inspiration for completing this book. I love you all from the deepest part of my heart.

Tawni and **Josh** -- Thanks for burning the midnight oil.

Jack and **Marsha Countryman** -- although we've spent limited time together, each time I'm around you guys I'm inspired to do more. Your wisdom, guidance, and counsel have been priceless.

Terence Rose -- My spiritual father and mentor for nearly a decade. Not to mention a loyal friend.

Bill Murdock -- Thanks for your input, especially the quotes.

Joe Phillips -- You helped me to get the ball "rollin'." Now it's your turn.

Don Eldred -- My buddy, my pal, my home away from home. Thanks, best friend.

Teresa Gitomer -- Thanks for your ideas and input. Especially your typing skills.

Matt Holt -- thanks for believing in us. I look forward to our next project together.

Rachel Russotto -- The countless hours spent without Jeffrey and me, the adding, subtracting, editing, re-editing, suggestions and changes, priceless. Jeffrey doesn't pay you enough. Then again, neither did I.

Tim Quinn, Todd Harvey, and Don Kernodle -- Your support and encouragement have been absolutely incredible. Thanks so much. You guys are awesome!

All my fans -- Without you, I'd still be delivering mail in Minneapolis. Thank you for your e-mails, support, encouragement, and prayers.

And to the rest of you, too many to name, who've made an impact on my life, a sincere Thank You. I'll never be the same.

A special note of thanks and gratitude to my co-author: Jeffrey, I can't even begin to tell you what your friendship means to me. What a journey it's been from the first time we met years ago when you said, "I hate your stinking guts," till now. Your consistent and persistent challenges over the years have brought me to a level of success I only dreamed of. This book, for example, years in the making, to see it come to fruition is such a blessing. Who would have thought the odd couple, Felix and Oscar (I'm definitely Oscar), a Jew and a gentile, coming together to collaborate on such a successful project? The Man Upstairs is definitely looking out for us. Your insight and intellect are such an inspiration. Your wit and humor bring merriment to my soul. I'm really looking forward to seeing what the future will hold for us.

ACKNOWLEDGMENTS: GITOMER

Books are not written. They are thought out, they are labored over, they are edited, they are reworked, and they seem to be almost a never-ending process. I could go back and change a hundred things inside this book, but I would never change the process by which the book was written. That was a labor of love.

I'm a writer, not an author. I love the process of writing, and I love the people I work with as the book emerges. First are the transcribers. Those who can type faster than I can, that help me capture thoughts. "Hey, Rachel! Can you type something for me?" "Hey, Teresa! Can you type something for me?" **Rachel Russotto** and **Teresa Gitomer** are always there for me. They translate my thoughts into data. I am grateful to them.

And Rachel has been the conscience of this book. Reading, editing, reading, editing, reading, editing. You get the idea. She has kept the Post-it note people in business. But it has been her hard work that has been the glue for this project. I acknowledge her and I thank her.

Nikita Koloff is the nicest, most gentle gentleman I know. He is a man of earth and a man of God. He is a dad, he is a friend, and he is a genuinely nice guy. Working with him has been a joy because it meant spending quality hours with him. Not just getting to hear his story, but getting to understand his soul. As much of a villain as his character was, that's how much of a great person he has become. Nikita Koloff is an inspiration that others can enjoy over and over. He has tapes of his sermons that you can buy on his website, www.nikitakoloff.com. Go there and buy one.

Mitchell Kearney has once again taken the supreme photograph. His ability to capture an image is an art.

Greg Russell has once again taken bland words on a sheet of paper and turned them into graphic art. He makes reading words pleasing to the eye. His ability to turn words into graphics is an art.

And I want to acknowledge all the wrestlers I have ever watched. As a fan I booed and cheered -- hoping the good guy would win. I have been a fan for almost fifty years. But it was not until I met Nikita Koloff, someone whom I hated, and I mean really hated, that I came to understand the meaning of predetermined outcomes. I want to acknowledge that those two words have played a major part in my own quest for success and have played a major part in keeping me a student.

And I would also like to thank my mom and dad who are watching from above.

About the Author, Nikita Koloff

Personal development leader, teacher, speaker, evangelist, author, husband, and dad

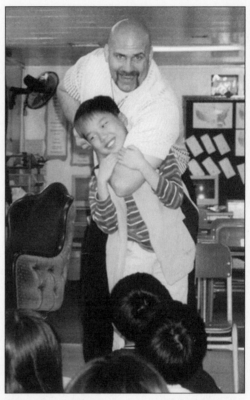

Nikita, a devoted husband, father, and man of God has striven to become the best he can possibly be by applying biblical principles in his life. He has now added public speaking to his list of accomplishments, conducting both motivational and inspirational seminars for businesses and corporations around the world.

He is very involved in humanitarian as well as missions work worldwide, having traveled to Africa, South America, Trinidad, Curacao, Moldova, Japan, Europe, Canada, and Singapore. He speaks in churches all over the world as well as primary, secondary, and collegiate school campuses and is very involved with various youth groups.

Demonstrating a proper rear chin lock in South Korea (2003). Working with kids is very enriching.

In order to arrive at a destination, one must have a road map. It is the intent of the author that this book offer a road map to help you along life's journey and arrive safely at your destination.

If you would like to inquire about Nikita Koloff's availability to speak at your church, school, or business, or if you would like to purchase additional books, t-shirts, autographed photos, or tapes, please contact the author at:

Nikita Koloff
P.O. Box 5598
Concord, NC 28027
nikita@nikitakoloff.com
www.nikitakoloff.com

Jeffrey Gitomer
Chief Executive Salesman

Author. Jeffrey Gitomer is the author of *The Sales Bible* and *Customer Satisfaction Is Worthless -- Customer Loyalty is Priceless*. After nearly twenty first-edition reprintings of *The Sales Bible*, the revised soft-bound business edition is still atop the bestseller chart. Jeffrey's books have sold more than 350,000 copies worldwide.

Over 100 presentations a year. Jeffrey gives seminars, runs annual sales meetings, and conducts training programs on selling and customer service. He has presented an average of 115 seminars a year for the past ten years.

Big Corporate Customers. Jeffrey's customers include Coca-Cola, Cingular Wireless, Hilton, Choice Hotels, Enterprise Rent-A-Car, Cintas, Milliken, NCR, *Financial Times*, Turner Broadcasting, Comcast Cable, Time Warner Cable, HBO, Ingram Micro, Wells Fargo Bank, BMW, Baptist Health Care, Blue Cross Blue Shield, Hyatt Hotels, Carlsburg Beer, Wausau Insurance, Northwestern Mutual, Sports Authority, GlaxoSmithKline, XEROX, A.C. Nielsen, Ricoh U.S., AT&T, Caterpillar, and hundreds of others.

In front of millions of readers every week. His syndicated column *Sales Moves* appears in more than eighty-five business newspapers and is read by more than 3,500,000 people every week.

And every month. Jeffrey's column appears in more than twenty-five trade publications and newsletters. Jeffrey has also been a contributor and featured expert in *Entrepreneur* and *Selling Power* magazines.

On the Internet. His three WOW web sites -- *www.gitomer.com*, *www.trainone.com*, and *www.knowsuccess.com* -- get as many as 5,000 hits a day from readers and seminar attendees. His state-of-the-art web-presence and e-commerce ability have set the standard among peers and has won huge praise and acceptance from customers.

Up Your Web-based Sales Training. A weekly streaming video (low cost/high value) sales-training lesson is now available on *www.trainone.com*. The content is pure Jeffrey -- fun, pragmatic, real world, and immediately implementable. This innovation is leading the way in the field of e-learning.

Sales Caffeine. A weekly "e-zine" sales wake-up call delivered every Tuesday morning to more than 85,000 subscribers free of charge. This allows us to communicate valuable sales information, strategies, and answers to sales professionals on a timely basis.

Sales Assessment Online. The world's first customized sales assessment. Renamed a "successment," this amazing sales tool will not only judge your selling skill level in twelve critical areas of sales knowledge, it will give you a diagnostic report that includes fifty mini-sales lessons as it rates your sales abilities and explains your customized opportunities for sales-knowledge growth. Aptly named "KnowSuccess" -- the company's mission is: *You can't know success until you know yourself.*

Award for Presentation Excellence. In 1997, Jeffrey was awarded the designation "Certified Speaking Professional" (CSP) by the National Speakers Association. The CSP award has been given less than 500 times in the past twenty-five years.

Buy Gitomer, Inc.
310 Arlington Avenue • Loft 329
Charlotte, North Carolina 28203
www.gitomer.com • 704/333-1112 • salesman@gitomer.com

INDEX

OTHER TITLES BY NIKITA KOLOFF & JEFFREY GITOMER

BY NIKITA KOLOFF

Breaking the Chains

BY JEFFREY GITOMER

The Sales Bible: The Ultimate Sales Resource

The Patterson Principles of Selling

**Customer Satisfaction Is Worthless,
Customer Loyalty Is Priceless:
How to Make Customers Love You, Keep Them
Coming Back and Tell Everyone They Know**

Jeffrey Gitomer's Little Red Book of Selling

Knock Your Socks Off Selling
by Jeffrey Gitomer and Ron Zemke

For Jeffrey Gitomer's seminars and
other great sales material, or for Internet
sales training information please call 704/333-1112.
www.gitomer.com
www.trainone.com

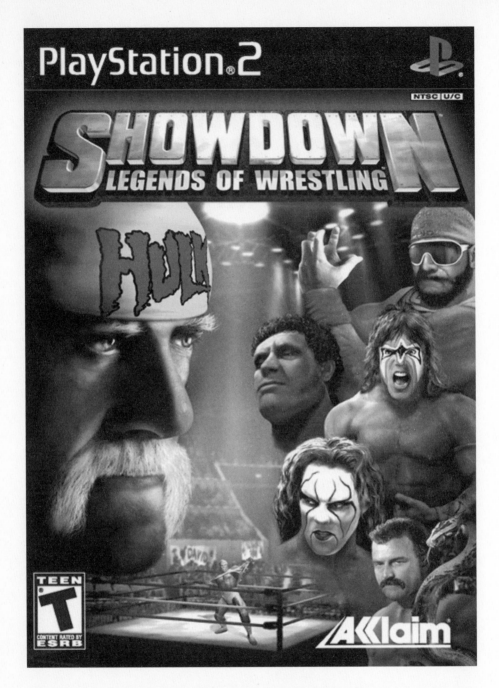

Thank you for purchasing *Wrestling with Success*. Be sure to also check out "The Russian Nightmare" Nikita Koloff in the exciting new video game from Acclaim titled SHOWDOWN: Legends of Wrestling. In Stores June 2004!